SO YOU WANT TO PLAY IN THE
NHL

SO YOU WANT TO PLAY IN THE
NHL

A GUIDE FOR YOUNG PLAYERS

DAN & JAY BYLSMA

CONTEMPORARY BOOKS

Library of Congress Cataloging-in-Publication Data

Bylsma, Dan, 1970–
   So you want to play in the NHL : a guide for young players / Dan and
Jay Bylsma.
     p.   cm.
    ISBN 0-8092-9952-6
    1. Bylsma, Dan, 1970–   2. Hockey players—United States—
Biography.   3. Fathers and sons—United States.   4. Achievement
motivation.   5. Bylsma, Jay M.   I. Bylsma, Jay M.   II. Title.
GV848.5.B95 A33   2001
796.962'092'273—dc21   00-31410
                                                 CIP

Cover design by Marc Paez
Cover photograph copyright © Debora Robinson
Interior design by Jennifer Locke

Published by Contemporary Books
A division of NTC/Contemporary Publishing Group, Inc.
4255 West Touhy Avenue, Lincolnwood (Chicago), Illinois 60712-1975 U.S.A.

Printed in the United States of America
International Standard Book Number: 0-8092-9952-6
01 02 03 04 05 MV 19 18 17 16 15 14 13 12 11 10 9 8 7 6 5 4 3 2 1

CONTENTS

FOREWORD TO PARENTS

I have to be honest with you up front; the title of this book is misleading. But if you were honest, you'd have to admit you might not have picked up the book if it was titled *So You're Not Going to Make the NHL, but Here's How to Enjoy Hockey Now and Life After Hockey Anyway and Learn Something About Life in the Process.* This is a book written by Dan Bylsma, a member of the Anaheim Mighty Ducks of the National Hockey League (NHL), and his father in which they relate important life lessons for aspiring kids. They use their experiences of Dan's journey to the NHL and what they've learned to give kids who play hockey (and for that matter, any kid who is passionate about any or all sports) answers to the questions they have about the game, about their chances of making it, and about some of the choices they will be faced with.

I played with Dan Bylsma for four seasons when he played for the Los Angeles Kings, and while I may be a household word for my ability to put the puck in the net, he should be a household word for his wisdom and insight about the game and what it takes to play it and his ability to identify and articulate the values that are important for kids playing the game.

This book will be required reading for my hockey playing son, and it should be required reading for every kid who aspires to play youth hockey. And it wouldn't be so bad if you read it, too.

Luc Robitaille

ACKNOWLEDGMENTS

We wish to thank the following young hockey players (h), parents (p), and/or siblings (s) of players whose suggestions motivated us to write this book and whose thoughtful input improved the manuscript.

Eric Gillingham (p), Toronto, Ontario

Seth Hawthorne (h), Spring Lake, Michigan

Zack (h) and Ed (p) Labine, St. Albert, Alberta

J. D. (p) and Vicki (p) Martin, Lenexa, Kansas

Daniel (h) and Laurie (s) Monteforte, Bushkill, Pennsylvania

Matthew (h), Shannon (h), Chris (h), and Scott (p) Moulson, Mississauga, Ontario

Chris (h) and Rich (p) Orlando, Ivyland, Pennsylvania

Mark Pawlowski (p), Mississauga, Ontario

Evan (h) and Mark K. (p) Stephens, Bessemer, Michigan

Travis (h), Terry (p), and Casey (p) Vayda, Bradenton, Florida

We are especially grateful to three professionals whose counsel and advice were invaluable: Lynn Deur, publisher at River Road Publications, whose editorial suggestions helped an older kid and a really old guy write a book for kids; Joseph Horrigan, Ph.D., weight and conditioning trainer for the Los Angeles Kings, for his wisdom and experience concerning weight training for young athletes; Thomas Spahn, Ed. D., child psychologist with Human Resource Associates of Grand Rapids, Michigan, and longtime youth hockey coach and player, for his review of and assistance with the material in Chapter 26.

INTRODUCTION

We were encouraged to write this book as the result of the wonderful response to our first book, *So Your Son Wants to Play in the NHL*. We hoped that book would serve as a guide for parents who had children who dreamed of playing in the NHL or any other professional sport as well as for kids who had such dreams. But over and over, the message came from both parents and kids, "I wish there was a book like this for kids."

So this book is for kids—that is, kids who dream of playing in the NHL, the NBA, the NFL, or in major league baseball. We encourage those dreams. We also encourage amateur sports because we think they are a great way to learn about life before the risky business of being a grownup comes around.

We hope you like the book. We hope you gain something from the things we learned from Dan's trip from Mite hockey to the NHL, including junior high, high school, college hockey, and the minors in the middle.

As you will see, this is a father and son book. Sometimes Dan (the son who has played more than 220 games with the Los Angeles Kings and now plays for the Anaheim Mighty Ducks of the NHL) will be writing and giving you the benefit of his experience. Sometimes Jay (Dan's father and sometimes his coach) will be writing and sharing his thoughts.

We think it will be useful for you to read our different points of view. Of course, you will want to read how Dan made it all the way to the NHL. Starting on our backyard ice rink with a lot of hard work and perseverance, he realized his dream of playing in the NHL—on a line with Wayne Gretzky, no less. And by the way, you need to get familiar with the word *perseverance*. It means to keep on trying, no matter how hard, no matter how long, no matter what, until you have reached a goal or finished a job. We use that word a lot and there's not really a smaller word that means the same thing.

Jay writes because it was his advice and guidance that helped Dan make it to the NHL, and helped four other children to successful careers. Maybe some of that same advice and guidance will be helpful to you, too.

1 | *WHO IS DAN BYLSMA?*

JAY

That's a good question to start with and as his father, I'm probably the most qualified person to introduce you to him. Dan is presently in his fifth season as a winger/centerman in the National Hockey League (NHL). As I like to say, he's Number 21 in the program, but Number 1 in my heart. But to say that Dan plays in the NHL doesn't say who he is, only that he has realized his childhood dream, perhaps the same dream you have to play in the NHL.

When he was three years old, Dan started skating on the rink our family made in our backyard. He has three older brothers who were good skaters, so you might imagine how hard Dan had to battle when playing in their games. No matter how old he was or how good he became, his brothers were always older and bigger than he was.

When Dan was six, I persuaded the leaders of the house leagues in the Muskegon (Michigan) Junior Hockey Program to allow him to play on a Squirt team that his brother Jon played on and that I coached. We didn't have Mite teams, but Dan was able to play at Squirt level because of all the skating he had done in our backyard.

Dan continued to play house leagues for several years, plus an occasional all-star game. We didn't have travel hockey in our area at that time. (House leagues are teams that take all players who sign up to play; they play all their games at one rink. Travel leagues are teams that have tryouts, choose the best players, and travel to other rinks to play other teams that also travel.) Also, I didn't think it was as important to play travel hockey as it was to get good grades in school and to attend church functions, so Dan probably would not have played travel hockey if it had been available. Education and religion more important than hockey? Sounds old-fashioned, I know. But I didn't know any better then. And hockey wasn't that important to our family. My kids played all the sports: baseball in the spring, golf in the summer, flag football and soccer in the fall. Hockey was the sport they played in the winter.

The high school Dan attended didn't have a hockey team, but in his freshman year he won the Michigan State High School Class D golf championship. The following spring, he made and started on the baseball team as a freshman and was a big part of the team winning the State Championship Finals. That year Dan's older brother Scott made the hockey team at Bowling Green State University (BGSU). I think that was when hockey became more than a recreational sport for Dan and the goal to play college hockey formed in his mind.

When Dan was a sophomore (he was 14, a Major Bantam), he ran out of competition in the house leagues in Muskegon, so we allowed him to play for the Grand Rapids Whalers AAA Major Midget Travel team. He did very well, leading the team in scoring. That exposure resulted in Dan being invited to the Michigan Select Midget Camp.

After the Midget Camp, we received a call from a Junior B Team in Canada with an invitation to join the team for the next season. It was a big decision because Dan would have to leave his high school, his family, and his friends. He decided it was a necessary step if he wanted to play college hockey.

Each spring Dan would come home after hockey ended and attend his old high school and play baseball. In his senior year Dan was selected to the all-state all-class "Dream Team" (the best player at each position in the state) as well as winning many regional baseball honors.

After playing Junior B hockey in Canada for his junior and senior years, he received offers for hockey scholarships from several schools and chose to attend BGSU to wear the number his older brother Scott had worn when he played there.

Dan was drafted by the Winnipeg Jets in his freshman year in college and went on to a respectable career at BGSU and was named to the Central Collegiate Hockey Association (CCHA) All-Academic team three times. (The CCHA All-Academic team is made up of the five hockey players in the league with the highest grade point average.)

When Dan graduated in 1992, he decided to try to play hockey professionally (his dream) instead of making use of his accounting degree (my dream for him). After leading Winnipeg's farm team (the Moncton Hawks) in scoring in the preseason, to his great disappointment he was released. All was not lost however; he went on to play in the East Coast Hockey League (ECHL) for the Greensboro Monarchs. He was a candidate for Rookie of the Year and was selected as the team's Most Valuable Player.

Dan was selected to attend the Anaheim Mighty Ducks first training camp, but disappointment struck again when he was released and sent back to Greensboro. In December he was called up to the Moncton Hawks, who were in last place in the league at the time. Partly because of Dan's penalty killing and leadership, the team began to win and went on to the Calder Cup finals before losing to the Portland Pirates in five games. Moncton's coach, Rob Laird, said that much of the team's success was because of Dan and his contagious work ethic, his positive attitude, and his inspirational leadership.

Dan then signed his first NHL contract with the L.A. Kings and went to their training camp but was sent down to the Phoenix Roadrunners. In his second year with the Roadrunners, he was called up to the Kings and played his first NHL game. Not only was playing in the NHL a big thrill, but it was even more thrilling because Dan got to play on a line with his childhood idol, Wayne Gretzky.

In the third year of his contract (1996–1997), Dan was a regular in the Kings lineup, playing in 79 of the 82 games that season. He was a member of the team's penalty killing unit, which set a team record of 87.2 percent efficiency that season, a percentage which ranked fifth best all time in the NHL record book.

At the end of the season, Dan was voted "Most Popular Player" by the Kings Booster Club, an honor he shared with Ian Laperriere, and he was a recipient with goalkeeper Byron Dafoe of the Kings "Community Service Award."

The Phoenix Roadrunners announced they would be ceasing operations as of the end of the 1996–1997 season. They also announced the selection of Dan for the All-Time Best Phoenix Roadrunner Team.

Dan began the following season with the Kings new International Hockey League (IHL) affiliate, the Long Beach Ice Dogs, but was recalled to the Kings after eight games and finished out the season with the Kings, playing in 65 games.

For the next season, Dan played up and down between the Kings (8 games) and the Ice Dogs (68 games). He was awarded the Unsung Hero Award by his Ice Dog teammates and the Kemper Award by the Ice Dog organization for professionalism on and off the ice. During the season, *So Your Son Wants to Play in the NHL*, a book cowritten by Dan and me, was published by Sleeping Bear Press in the United States and by McClelland & Stewart in Canada. That book tells of Dan's journey to the NHL in much more detail.

Dan was on the King's roster for the entire 1999–2000 season. He played in 68 regular season and 3 play-off games. For the 2000–2001 season Dan signed to play for the Anaheim Mighty Ducks.

As you can see, the road to the NHL was a long and difficult one. Dan's had lots of experiences and has overcome a lot of disappointments along the way. With this book he hopes he can pass along some of what he's learned to you.

2 | WHY PLAY SPORTS AT ALL?

SPORTS IS THE TOY DEPARTMENT OF HUMAN LIFE.

—HOWARD COSELL

JAY

An important question to consider at the beginning is "Why play sports at all?" Why do kids get involved in pick-up games in their backyards and why do they join organized programs like Little League Baseball and youth hockey? For kids the answers to why they play pick-up games are simple: you do it to have fun, to pass the time during after-school hours and during school vacations, and to do what the other kids are doing. There are good reasons why thoughtful parents also encourage these pick-up games. They know you will be learning things that will help you physically and emotionally as you grow up and when you're an adult.

Playing pick-up games

- keeps you fit
- helps you develop coordination, which gives you better control of your body
- helps you form a closer bond with your brothers and sisters
- helps you make new friends
- helps you learn to develop teamwork and to work within a group
- teaches you how to resolve conflicts deciding who plays on what team, what the batting order will be, and whether a call is "Out" or "Safe" on close plays at first base
- keeps you occupied in a healthy activity instead of hanging out at the mall or becoming a couch potato

So parents provide you with the equipment (like bats and balls and skates and sticks) and allow you to destroy the grass in the backyard to encourage and enable you to play because these games help in your development as a person.

Some of the same reasons have caused parents and other adults to develop organized programs like USA Hockey, Little League Baseball, Pop Warner Football, Gus Macker Three-on-Three Basketball, and sports in school from junior high to college. These programs were created and continue at the cost of a lot of money and volunteer time. The reasons are similar.

Organized youth sports programs

- allow more kids to have the fun of playing sports
- provide adult coaching and teaching so young players can learn the fundamentals and rules of the sport
- teach kids how to play on a team and how important cooperative effort is for a team to reach a goal
- teach kids how to handle and cope with stress. One little player standing at the plate facing nine or ten players who are trying to get him out and a pitcher who is throwing a hard ball at him is very scary at first. Learning to handle that fear and resulting stress and perhaps overcoming it is very beneficial and will help kids learn how to handle scary situations later in life

Nearly all of the reasons listed above can be lumped into one category—to teach you life lessons. These lessons help you learn what the world is like before you have to face it as an adult. They will help prepare you to live a more productive and happy life. And the most important reason you play sports is to have fun!

3 | WHOSE DREAM IS IT TO PLAY IN THE NHL?

THE DREAM MUST BE YOURS, OR THE JOURNEY
WILL BE A NIGHTMARE.

—*DAN*

DAN

I can remember my earliest games played in the big back-yard of our home. These were games in which my brothers and I pretended to be our favorite sports heroes. When we played hockey I wanted to be Wayne Gretzky, one of my brothers wanted to be Phil Esposito (the first NHLer to score 70 goals), another brother was a goalie and pretended he was Tony Esposito (called Tony O because he had so many shutouts), and so on. Once, as Wayne Gretzky, I took the puck end-to-end and scored the game-winning goal—top shelf, glove side—against Tony O in overtime to win the Stanley Cup. And after our back-yard games, I fell exhausted into bed. Sleep would come quickly and I would score again to win the Stanley Cup in my dreams. (And to be truthful, that's still a dream of mine.)

What I didn't know back then was how much desire, practice, hard work, and perseverance (remember that means to keep on trying no matter what) it actually would take to make the dream of playing in the NHL with Wayne Gretzky come true. I didn't realize there were about a million kids just like me on ice ponds and rinks all around the world with the same dream. And to make it to the NHL, I would have to become better than just about every one of them.

If your dream is to come true, all the desire, practice, hard work, and perseverance must be yours, no one else's. And the dream must truly be yours. It cannot be the dream of your coach, your father, your mother, your brother, or anyone else. No amount of hoping, dreaming, encouraging, or nagging by someone else gives you the desire and perseverance it will take to make it.

The dream must be yours, or the journey will be a nightmare.

JAY

You may think it's strange that we ask if it's really *your* dream to play in the NHL. But it's a good question. We have seen the results when parents dreamed their child would play in the NHL, but that dream wasn't shared by the child. In every case the results have not been what the parents wished for, and sometimes it has been the source of trouble between the child and the parents.

Sometimes young people play sports because they think their parents will like them more. I did that. My father was one of the best basketball players in our city when he was in high school. So, as his son, I was expected to be a basketball player, and my father pushed me to follow in his footsteps. But I didn't like basketball enough to want to work at it and I was cut from the high school team. I was ashamed and felt I had let my father down terribly. He thought I had let him down, too.

I now realize that playing high school basketball wasn't as important for my growth and development as a person as what I did instead of playing basketball. I joined the high school debate team. Debate taught me to think logically, to express myself clearly, and to think and speak on my feet, skills that helped me be a successful businessman. It has even helped me write books. Unfortunately, my father's bitterness over my being cut from the basketball team prevented him from being proud of my accomplishments as a debater. The basketball team got beat in the state district tournaments that year, while the debate team went to the state semifinals.

Sometimes parents' hopes and dreams push their children to practice and play games beyond the point that it is fun for the child and even to the point where a child can't stand the game anymore. That's called *burnout,* and when the child experiences burnout, the sport becomes a chore and drudgery and no longer fun.

I once heard Sparky Anderson, a member of baseball's Hall of Fame and former coach of the Cincinnati Reds and the Detroit Tigers, give this advice to a parent: "Your child will make it to the Major Leagues *in spite of* what you do for him, not *because of* what you do for him." What Mr. Anderson was saying is that the dream and the effort to make the dream come true has to come from you. If you have what it takes, there's nothing your parents can to do stop it. The opposite is just as true. If you don't have the dream and are not willing to spend the effort, there's nothing your parents can do to see to it that you make it.

You may be reading this book because you want to become a better hockey player. My message to you is that if you love hockey more than anything in the world, you have one of the basic things it takes to make it to the NHL. If you don't, you can still play the game for fun (I played for fun until I was 55 years old). You may change and have what it takes when you get older. But whether it's hockey like Dan or debating like me, if you want to be happy and successful in life, find something you love and do it the best you can.

Dan still loves the game, even after all the practices he's been through, all the conditioning in the summer time, and the nearly 750 games in college and professional hockey he's played in. I think that's because the dream of playing in the NHL was not mine for him. I never thought, never hoped, never dreamed he would play in the NHL. That may be one of the important reasons he made it—it was his dream and his alone.

WHAT'S THE MOST IMPORTANT THING YOU CAN DO TO MAKE IT TO THE NHL?

4

> IGNORANCE IS A LOT LIKE ALCOHOL: THE MORE YOU HAVE OF IT, THE LESS YOU ARE ABLE TO SEE ITS EFFECT ON YOU.
>
> —JAY

DAN

When I was growing up, my parents told me over and over again the importance of getting a good education. I was expected to do my best in school and go to college and get a degree, just like my older brothers had before me and my sister would after me. But I didn't know just how important it was to be a good student and get good grades until I was in high school and had the opportunity to go to Canada and play Junior B hockey. I learned that Canadian high schools didn't want to take foreign hockey players into their schools unless they were good students. In other words, without good grades, I couldn't have accepted the invitation to play Junior hockey in Canada. Although I didn't know it at the time, getting good grades was my first step in getting to the NHL.

Because of my success in Junior B hockey in Canada, I was recruited by a number of college coaches. Some people think that if you're really good at hockey, colleges will give you a scholarship regardless of your grades. That may be true if your last name is Gretzky, but for the rest of us grades and college entrance exam scores are as important as the number of times you put the puck in the net. Good grades alone won't get you the hockey scholarship, but bad grades will keep you from being offered a scholarship or even being accepted into college.

The high school I attended in Canada sent all the hockey players' grades to the team's General Manager (GM). If a college coach called the GM to inquire about a player, he would always ask what the player's grades were. Why? Because colleges have admission standards. If the player's grades or test scores didn't meet his school's entrance requirements, the coach lost interest in that player. The number of scholarships a coach can give out is limited. He can't afford to waste a scholarship on a player who can't get good enough grades to stay eligible or, worse, who flunks out of school.

I was very happy that I had worked hard and gotten good grades. It helped me win a coveted full-ride scholarship to Bowling Green State University where I played for four years for the Fighting Falcons. Collegiate athletics is the farm system for almost every professional sport, particularly in the United States. And what do you need to get into college? Good grades!

Good grades are one of the most important things you need to get to the NHL. Realistically, they may be more important for you than being the best player on your team. Why? Because you are more likely to become a doctor than an NHLer. If you don't believe me, count the number of doctors listed in your city's phone directory. Compare that to the number of NHLers that have come from your city.

A very small number of exceptional players like Wayne Gretzky know they are going to make the NHL from the time they are 16. For other players like myself, it was very important to play at the college level. Joey Nieuwendyk, Adam Oates, and Paul Kariya, who improved slowly every year, didn't make it to the NHL until later on at age 21 or older. For us, the extra time we had to improve our skills at college was an important part of our making it to the NHL.

So then, what's one of the most important things you can do to get to the NHL? Get good grades in school!

JAY

Every time a college coach or recruiter talked to Dan's mother or me about Dan, the first questions they would ask us were "What are Dan's ACT or SAT [college entrance exams] scores?" and "How are Dan's grades?" We were very pleased that Dan had very good grades and high enough college admission test scores to qualify for any college hockey program.

But there are other reasons for working hard and getting the best grades you can. Education is a chance to go from a puddin' head to a person who has been exposed to the greatest ideas of Western civilization: its literature, its sciences, its music, its art, and its history. By working hard in school and doing your best, you're taking advantage of a precious opportunity to expand your mind and your imagination.

How will this help you get to the NHL? There are practical applications besides enabling you to get into college. Education teaches you how to think, study, and analyze things. When you are coming down on the goalie two on one with a teammate, can you study and analyze the situation and think of a solution in the split second it takes for the play to develop? Education teaches you to think and analyze.

Education teaches you how to think and speak clearly when you need to talk about a problem to your coach or a referee or a league official. Education will help you understand your contract when you do get to the NHL. You will be better able to express your thoughts to the media after a game or when you have to speak after winning the Conn Smythe trophy. Education will help you handle your finances when you get to the NHL.

Also, there is life after hockey, and for most of us that comes sooner rather than later. A good education may help you get a good job after hockey. Education gives you knowledge and dispels ignorance. So what's the most important preparation for the NHL and for life after hockey? Get good grades in school.

Ignorance is a lot like alcohol: the more you have of it, the less you are able to see its effect on you. Think about that.

5 | WHAT'S THAT FIRE IN MY BELLY?

WE ARE TOLD THAT TALENT CREATES ITS OWN OPPORTUNITIES. BUT IT SOMETIMES SEEMS THAT INTENSE DESIRE CREATES NOT ONLY ITS OWN OPPORTUNITIES, BUT ITS OWN TALENTS.

—*ERIC HOFFER*

DAN

I was the youngest of four boys in my family. From the time I can first remember, my brothers were always playing sports in our backyard. It was baseball in the spring, golf in the summer, football in the fall, and hockey in the winter. And while they played for fun, they also played to win.

When they allowed me to join their games, I soon learned that it was fun to play, it was more fun to be good at the games we played, but it was the most fun to win. Luckily, my brothers and the neighbor kids we played with had a sense of fair play. They chose fair teams so that sometimes my team won and sometimes my team lost. But I found I would rather win than lose. In fact, I hated to lose. I would always try my best to do what it took to win.

Winning makes you feel good about yourself. It is an accomplishment and contributes to your sense of self-worth. Doing your best or achieving the silver medal can also give you good feelings about yourself. But usually, winning the game or the gold medal feels a little bit better. It's the way we are made as humans.

Wanting to win, wanting to feel that high that comes from winning, and wanting to prove you and your team were better than someone else or some other team is known as being competitive. So there are three things that make up competitiveness: wanting to win, wanting that good feeling that comes from winning, and wanting to know who's better.

In some people competitiveness is very strong, like a fire in their belly. For others it's not so important. Competitiveness is not just found in athletics. You will experience it in school and later as you grow up in the adult world.

Competitiveness can be a very positive thing, helping you be the best you can be. It encourages you to practice in order to get better and to try harder at a sport and thereby help you win. It can encourage you to study hard to get on the honor role (another form of winning) or to practice your trombone so you can be first chair in your section of the school band.

Competitiveness can also lead to bad behavior. You may want to win so much that you consider cheating to win or to get good grades. However, if you win or get good grades because you cheated, *you* will be cheated as well. You will have only one of the three things you competed for. You may have won, but you won't have the good feeling that comes from winning. You really won't know if you or your team was better than the other person or team.

Competitiveness can help you achieve goals and grades that you would not attain if you didn't have a fire in your belly. But competitiveness is also like a regular fire. Be careful to control it and not let it control you.

JAY

I agree with Dan that competition is a good thing. When Dan was in third grade, the school he attended gave one of two possible marks: *S* for Satisfactory or *U* for Unsatisfactory. He responded by doing just enough work to get an *S* in each of his subjects.

When Dan entered the fourth grade, he went to a different school where they used the *A*, *B*, *C*, *D*, and *F* grading system. He worked much harder because he wanted to get the best grade he could. As a result he learned more. In a more competitive marking system, he was challenged to win a higher grade.

While growing up, Dan played a lot with his brothers who were older and better than he was. Both Dan and I believe that this high level of competition forced him to work harder and try harder if he wanted to play as an equal with his brothers. Learning this at a young age is one of the important reasons he made it to the NHL.

Just as making it to the NHL is very competitive, life is very competitive. Just like only a few players make it to the NHL, only a few students get all *A*s on their report cards. Only a few kids make the all-star team. Only one trombonist gets to be first chair. Only a few make it to college. Only a few people get the very best jobs or become doctors or lawyers.

To make it to the NHL you have to have a fire in your belly. That is, you have to want it passionately. The same is true with getting all *A*s, making it on the all-star team, being first chair, getting to college, or becoming a doctor. If you don't care passionately, or you care less than passionately, or you are careless about your opportunities, then you must be willing to accept less than the best you can be.

Being less than the best you can be would be a tragedy.

6 WHAT'S SO IMPORTANT ABOUT RULES?

> NO ONE HAS EVER SCORED THE WINNING GOAL
> FROM THE PENALTY BOX.
>
> —JAY

DAN

When I was playing Kid's League Baseball (our town's version of Little League), my father was my coach. Knowing the rules was always a big thing with him. I remember one game in which we had a one-run lead and the other team loaded the bases in the last half of the last inning with one out. The batter hit a ground ball to the second baseman, but the runner from first base got hit with the ball before it got to the second baseman.

During the play, two runs scored and the other team whooped it up. They thought they had won. But the umpire ruled that the interference caused a dead ball and the runner who got hit with the ball was out. The other runners had to return to their bases, and the batter was safe on first. That all sounded reasonable and the other team still saw a victory in sight.

However, my dad knew the rule that if a runner interferes with a ball that was a potential double play, two are out, the runner that interfered and the runner closest to home plate. The game was therefore over, and we won because my father knew the rules.

Knowing the rules can not only help you win, but can prevent you from doing things that will hurt your chances of winning. Going offside on a three-on-one rush in hockey is an obvious example.

Some rules are made to give everyone an equal chance of winning (like the number of players allowed on the ice). Some are in place to control the game (like the length of the periods), and some are there to prevent injury (like high sticking). Violation of the rules has consequences ranging from stopping the play (like offside), to allowing the other team an advantage (like a power play or a penalty shot), to being taken out of the game temporarily (like having to serve a penalty), to being thrown out of the game (a game misconduct).

Knowing the rules is so important that I don't think you can really play any sport well without knowing them.

JAY

While Dan is right about the importance of knowing and following the rules to enable you to play well and to win, there is another reason for learning and following the rules. Just like there are rules in sports, there are rules in life. Just like there are penalties in sports for breaking the rules, there are also penalties in life for breaking the rules. Life's penalties, however, may be far more unpleasant than two minutes in the penalty box.

I encouraged my children to play sports and I encourage you to participate as well because sports are a lot more than a healthy alternative to being a couch potato or a video game wizard. Sports are a very good way to learn about what life is all about before the penalties become too severe or painful. Sports give you a glimpse of what life is like.

Using hockey as the example, let's compare sports to life for just a moment. In hockey you take into the rink all the equipment you have, all the practice, all the knowledge about the game and its rules. It's the same in life. You bring your knowledge and experience to whatever task or activity you undertake. In hockey you have coaches that teach you and tell you what to do. In life you have parents, teachers, and ministers or priests or rabbis who teach you and tell you what to do and how to live, that is, to give you a moral compass.

In hockey, there are referees to enforce the rules and give out penalties just as there are policemen and judges to enforce the law. Punishment in hockey likely means the penalty box. In life breaking the rules may result in a fine or even a jail term if the offense is serious enough. Breaking the rules in your job can result in being fired.

What you can learn through sports is that practice, hard work, listening to coaches, and knowing the rules will help you avoid the penalty box and will lead to more successes than being lazy, ignoring the advice of coaches, and breaking the rules. No one has ever scored the winning goal from the penalty box.

Sports, then, give us a bird's-eye view of life. And the neat thing about them is that they teach you important lessons at a time when a wrong decision or a mistake will not be costly. As you grow older, and you give up the game of hockey for the game of life, the cost of making mistakes and bad decisions can become far greater.

7 WHAT'S A MORAL COMPASS?

CONSCIENCE IS THE INNER VOICE, WHICH WARNS US
THAT SOMEONE MIGHT BE LOOKING.

—H. L. MENCKEN

DAN

When people go hiking in a strange place, they often take a compass along with them. A compass doesn't tell you where you are, but it always points north. If you know which way is north, you can tell what direction you need to travel to get where you're going. A compass, then, is a reliable tool that helps you decide which way to go.

A moral compass is not a device. It is a system of beliefs that helps you make decisions about how to live your life. It helps you decide what is the right thing to do and what may be wrong or harmful to you.

Where do you get a moral compass? Primarily from your parents. They are the first ones to tell you what is right and wrong. Parents tell you things to keep you safe, such as "don't touch the hot stove" and "don't play in the street." Later they may tell you it's wrong to lie, use bad language, cheat, or show disrespect to others. When you become a teenager, their instructions may include warnings about not stealing, not using alcohol or drugs, and other more serious issues.

I heard those lectures from my parents, too. I was eight when I learned the one about not lying and stealing. My father questioned me about some baseball cards I had stolen from a local convenience store. After lying myself into a hole I couldn't get out of, I found myself in the family car with my father driving me back to the store. There I had to apologize to a stern-faced manager who decided, at what appeared to me to be the last moment, not to call the police.

Back at home, my parents decided that one way to clean out a mouth that would speak such lies was with liquid dishwashing detergent. A Palmolive cocktail and the threat of a long-term jail sentence helped me understand that lying and stealing had unpleasant consequences. The experience helped shape my personal moral compass.

Where do parents get their moral compass? Primarily from *their* parents. But most people's moral compass is shaped by their religious traditions. Christians, for example, are influenced by priests, pastors, from church services, and the Bible. People of the Jewish faith listen to their rabbis, attend synagogue, and study the Torah. Muslims are influenced by attending the mosque and studying the Koran.

In these and other traditions, there are spiritual leaders who minister to their people using a sacred text. There is the common element of God, the creator of the universe who has revealed a moral code of conduct in these sacred texts. My parents are Christians, so the Bible and the Ten Commandments shape their moral compass.

As far back as I can remember, my parents attended church regularly and we kids had to go along. They thought it was more important for us to be good people than to be good hockey players. So if hockey interfered with church or youth group activities, I didn't play hockey. Once in a while, however, they let me skip church for a very important game.

Attending church was not my favorite thing to do. I thought it would be far more fun to be skating at the ice rink than counting the organ pipes in the front of the church, which is what I did when the sermon got too long. But now I understand how important it has been in shaping my moral compass. Why? Because I believe God wants good for his children and not evil, and evil is often the result of not obeying the moral code or as I like to say, of ignoring one's moral compass.

An example of this is a 15-year-old young man from my hometown who recently stole a car, filled up the tank, drove away without paying, got involved in drinking, began speeding, ran a red traffic signal, lost control of the car, and crashed into another car, killing the young woman driving it. He stole, drank under age, disobeyed the traffic laws, and caused the death of an innocent person. In the process, he ruined his own life and caused terrible grief for his family and the family of the young woman. Wrong actions in this case had obvious terrible consequences.

Not so obvious is the harm that comes from cheating, lying, and disobeying the rules at home or school, but these lead to the loss of your integrity, your self-respect, and your good name. I wish none of that harm for the people I care about, and I think the person we should each care most about is ourself. Having and obeying a moral compass will help you make good decisions, live a quality life, and avoid destructive behavior that most certainly will be harmful to you and perhaps to others.

8 WHAT'S SO IMPORTANT ABOUT BEING A TEAM PLAYER?

SHINNY IS NOT A PROFESSIONAL SPORT.

—JAY

DAN

When I was playing as a little kid, there were always one or two players in the league who were outstanding skaters and stick handlers. They could skate around everyone and dangle forever in front of the goalie. We all were envious of their skills and often dreaded playing against them.

My father usually didn't try to get that type of player on his team. Instead he always emphasized that hockey was a team sport. He would say, "When you can skate faster than you can pass the puck, then you don't have to pass the puck. Until then, pass the puck."

I think I learned to be a team player because I almost always played with older players, beginning in the backyard with my brothers. Because everyone else was older,

I had to pass the puck every chance I got or I got hammered, either because my opponent was bigger than I was or because the guys on my team would rag on me if I didn't. When the choice is pass the puck or pick yourself out of a snow bank, you pass the puck.

I learned what *fun* it could be to be a team player when I played on a team with a friend, Tommy Ferguson. My dad said that if we could turn Tommy into a scorer, we had a chance to win the league championship, even though we did not have the best players. He put me on a line with Tommy and it worked. Tommy led the league in scoring with 18 goals in 12 games and I had 21 assists. You can see from his goals and my assists that scoring and winning was a "we" thing, a team thing.

I remember it was as much fun to see the joy that Tommy experienced in scoring all those goals as scoring them myself. And my dad was right; we had ten wins, one loss, one tie, and won the league championship, mostly because Tommy Ferguson scored all those goals.

I think if I had tried to do all the scoring myself, we might not have won the championship. It reinforced what I already knew—that by working as a team we could win more games than if each person did his own thing.

JAY

One of the biggest tragedies in any team sport is a good player who doesn't understand the importance of being a team player. I have seen many players with outstanding skills who were not effective because either they thought that they could win the game by themselves or that their teammates weren't good enough to help get the win. If you watch pickup basketball games on the playgrounds of New York, you will see dozens of players who could probably beat Scottie Pippen or Karl Malone one-on-one. But those players are not in the NBA because they can't play as part of a team.

I always enjoyed coaching against these players. We called them "hot dogs" or "shinny players," and they would help me teach my players the importance of team play. They wouldn't pass the puck when they should have—they would shoot the puck themselves when they should have passed it to an open man. We could plan our defense accordingly and often a group of guys with teamwork could beat an opponent who relied on a hot dog to win for them.

It's important to develop into a team player because as you grow older the players get bigger, stronger, and better and you will have more and more trouble being a one-man show. As the teams you play on become older, your coaches will generally be more experienced and knowledgeable. They will have game plans with defenses designed to shut down the hot dog. As a result, many coaches will avoid choosing a hot dog–type player for their team because they know a hot dog is as easy to coach against as a hot dog with mustard and pickles is to eat.

There is another reason why it is important to learn to be a team player. Hockey is a game, not a show. You need to understand and play the game, not put on a show. If you do not learn this lesson, you will gain a reputation that will not serve you well. People who really understand hockey will say, "The kid's got great skills, but he doesn't understand the game."

There is one last reason why it is important to learn to be a team player. Shinny is not a professional sport. There is no NSL (National Shinny League).

9 EVERYONE SAYS I'LL NEVER MAKE IT

KEEP AWAY FROM PEOPLE WHO TRY TO BELITTLE YOUR AMBITIONS. SMALL PEOPLE ALWAYS DO THAT, BUT THE REALLY GREAT ONES MAKE YOU FEEL THAT YOU, TOO, CAN BECOME GREAT.

—MARK TWAIN

DAN

If I had quit the first time someone told me I wouldn't make it to play college hockey, much less make it to the NHL, I would have quit when I was a Major Bantam. From the time I began playing organized hockey, I was not recognized as a person who was good enough to "make it." There were always players who most people thought were better than I was. There were usually players who scored more goals than I did. I was never the talk of the league.

Although I led my AAA Midget team in scoring as a Major Bantam, my assistant coach said I was too slow and not strong enough to play Juniors. I led my Junior team in scoring, yet my Juniors coach admits that he never thought I would play in the NHL. I'm sure Jerry York, my college coach, didn't think I would make it to the NHL either. Apparently neither did the Winnipeg Jets' coaches. After they drafted me in the sixth round, 102nd overall, they didn't think enough of me to offer me a contract when I got out of college.

I can't fault these people because there were times when I doubted it myself. Even my father *never* dreamed I'd make it. So if people tell you that you won't make it, remember two things. First, most of the people who tell you that you won't make it didn't "make it" themselves and are likely poor judges of what it takes to "make it." Second, even people who have made it can't always tell who will succeed.

The general managers, coaches, and scouts who are the best minds in hockey conduct the NHL draft. Some first round draft picks never make it to the NHL and some tenth rounders become superstars, like my former teammate from the L.A. Kings Luc Robitaille (171st overall) who passed Rocket Richard on the all-time-scoring NHL list. Even some players who never get drafted go on to become superstars, like Dino Ciccerelli and Adam Oates. Jason Allison, the Boston Bruins' leading scorer, was cut from his Major Bantam team. Other players' parents in PeeWee used to say, "Oh no! Not *that* kid again," when the Mississauga (Canada) Reps coach put a little kid named Brendan Shanahan on the ice.

Not many people gave Todd Reirden, my college teammate at Bowling Green (and instructor at my hockey camp) any chance of making it to the NHL. He struggled in the ECHL, the AHL (American Hockey League), the IHL and after a few games in the NHL with Edmonton in the 1998–1999 season, he was sent down to their AHL affiliate at the end of the 1999–2000 training camp. But St. Louis picked Todd up and he had a spectacular season with the Blues, scoring lots of points and a very high plus/minus and played as Chris Pronger's linemate. (Plus/minus measures a player's effectiveness. A player gets a plus when he is on the ice when his team scores an even strength goal—"even strength" means there are six players on a side. He gets a minus if he is on the ice when the opposing team scores an even strength goal.)

It's best not to listen to anyone who says you can't make it. Only you can decide if you make it or not.

JAY

Whether or not you accomplish your goal, and that goal may be to play college or NHL hockey, will largely be determined by how hard you work and how long you can persevere in your attempt. So when a coach or someone else says you can't make it, what they really are saying is that you won't work hard enough, or that you will not persevere long enough to make it. Only you know how much you want it, how hard you are willing to work, and how long you can persevere in following your dream.

When Dan was playing for Greensboro in the East Coast Hockey League, he was near his brother Jon, who was going to law school at the University of North Carolina. Jon would take trips to see Dan play. I remember Jon calling home one day and reporting on a recent game and a visit with Dan. During our conversation Jon said, "That poor kid actually thinks he's going to make it to the NHL! From Greensboro! I didn't have the heart to burst his bubble." Dan's own brother didn't believe he would make it, either.

So don't be discouraged if someone says you'll never make it. They don't decide it for you; your fate is in your hands. And remember, they said it about Dan, Luc, Dino, Adam, Jason, Brendan, and Todd, too.

WHAT ARE MY CHANCES OF MAKING IT TO "THE SHOW"?

10

> FAILURE AFTER LONG PERSEVERANCE IS MUCH GRANDER THAN
> NEVER TO HAVE A STRIVING GOOD ENOUGH
> TO BE CALLED A FAILURE.
>
> —*GEORGE ELIOT*

JAY

Honestly?

They are somewhere between very slim and very, very slim.

You have to remember that hockey is an international sport. So you are competing not only with kids from the United States and Canada, but from most of the countries of Europe and the former Soviet Union as well. That means you will have to be one of the best hockey players in the world to make it to the NHL.

Currently there are about 150 U.S.-born players in the NHL. There are about 400,000 young players in organized youth hockey in the United States and about another 100,000 playing in other programs, such as high school or college, and in Canada. So statistically the chance that one U.S.-born player makes it to the NHL is one in 3,333. That's the same as saying you not only need to be the best player on your team, but you need to be better than all the other players on 200 other teams as well.

The odds are worse in baseball. There are about 4.5 million kids in amateur baseball programs around the world. There are about 700 major league players. This means that only one in 6,666 kids playing baseball will make it to the Major Leagues. If your Little League team is fortunate enough to make it to the Little League World Series, the chances improve, but not enough so you should start looking for an agent. Only 21 of the 1,530 players who have played in the championship game of the Little League World Series eventually made it to the Major Leagues.

So, if you're the best Squirt in your city, don't rest on that. Remember there are some Squirt-age players who are the best PeeWees somewhere else, and there are some Squirt players in Russia and Sweden who could play Midgets in our country.[1]

This is why when Dan was growing up I never thought or dreamed he would make it to the NHL, the

---

[1] In the spring of 1999, I toured Europe on a team of select PeeWees and Bantams assembled by Shawn Killian of Plant Hockey Skills Camps. Mr. Bylsma is right about the skill of some of the kids in other countries. I've seen them. We played a team of select PeeWees from Russia. We played against them, but couldn't catch them. We rarely touched the puck. No foolin'. We got thumped 14–0." —Evan Stephens, Bessemer, MI

Major Leagues, or the PGA Tour even though he was very good in hockey, baseball, and golf. I knew the chances of making it were very slim, if not impossible. So I insisted that his main responsibility was to get a good education because it is more important to have the best grades on your hockey team than to be the best player. Why? As Dan said before, more doctors will come out of your hockey program than NHL players will—a lot more.

I'd like to add that you can count all the professional athletes that have come out of your city: NBA players, NFL players, Major League Baseball players, and PGA Tour players, from the present to as far back as your grandfather can remember. The total won't come close to the number of doctors in your city today. I knew Dan had a far better chance to become a doctor, a dentist, an accountant, or an engineer than to make it to the NHL. And I knew for sure that their careers lasted longer than the careers of even the best NHLers.

I never laughed at my childrens' dreams to be the next Wayne Gretzky or Al Kaline or Jack Nicklaus, although I might have smiled at the thought. Still, I knew they would certainly need a job, and there was a good chance they would get married and become parents themselves. So I tried to prepare them for life. That preparation was to give them a moral compass, a good education, a strong family for support, and a good work ethic. That's what I knew they needed to be good people. I didn't know one of them would apply it to the NHL.

DAN

While it's important that you understand what my dad is saying, you have to understand that he went to college for accounting and finance; he works with and understands numbers and statistics. So while he is right that anybody's chances of making it to the NHL or Major League Baseball are very slim, you are not *anybody*. You're *somebody*. And you want to know what your chances are.

I'd like to change what my father says just a little. He said you have to be *better* than a lot of other kids to make it to "The Show." I'd like to tell you that you have to *work harder and longer* than a lot of other kids to make it to "The Show."

I'll be the first to admit that at every level that I played there were players who were more talented and had better skills than I had. There were a lot of college players who were more talented and had better skills than I did who didn't make it to the NHL. Why did I make it and not them? Because I worked harder, tried harder, wanted it more, and stuck with it longer than they did. And this is important for you to know because working harder, trying harder, desiring it passionately, and sticking with it longer are things that are within your power to control *regardless of your talent.*

You decide how hard you practice. You decide how hard you try. Only you know how much you want it, and how long you are willing to pursue your dreams. Only you will decide if you will become the *anyone* in my father's statistics or if you will be a *somebody* who dreamed the dream and worked, tried, desired, and persevered to turn the dream into a reality.

A famous philosopher of the twentieth century, a self-educated man named Eric Hoffer, once said, "We are told that talent creates its own opportunities. But it sometimes seems that intense desire creates not only its own opportunities, but its own talents."

My father has a similar saying. He says, "It takes three things to be successful: talent, hard work, and perseverance. And the greatest of these is not talent."

Those are quotations you can hang on your locker or put up on the bulletin board in your room.

11 | HOW HARD DO I HAVE TO WORK TO MAKE IT?

> IF YOU WANT TO MAKE IMPRESSIONS IN THE SANDS OF TIME,
> WEAR WORK BOOTS.
>
> —AUTHOR UNKNOWN

DAN

I said in the last chapter that realizing your dream, whether it be playing in the NHL or becoming a doctor, takes hard work. So now you want to know how much hard work.

Well, I have bad news and good news. The bad news is that the hard work is like moving a mountain with your hands. The good news is that you only have to do it one rock at a time. Your tryout camp for the NHL or the NFL isn't going to happen tomorrow, so you have time to start to move your mountain. How do you do that? Let me share with you how I did it.

First, I played every chance I got. My family built an ice rink in our backyard. It was big enough so we could play serious four-on-four games. As long as my homework and chores got done, I participated in every single one of those games in the backyard. I played against much bigger and better kids, so I had to work very hard to play up to their level. And if there was no one to play with, I played by myself. Sometimes I had to shovel the snow off the pond alone, but I never wanted to pass up an opportunity to play.

Second, whenever I had a practice, I skated as hard as I could. I tried to be the first one over and back on skating drills. I didn't cheat on the stops. Whenever I had a game, I tried as hard as I could and worked as hard as I could. When it was possible, I followed the Rule of Fifteen. I would get on the ice 15 minutes early and stay 15 minutes after the practice was over. If the practice were one hour long, I would have practiced for 50 percent longer than my teammates. After two practices, I would have practiced an hour longer than my teammates.

Third, if there were conditioning drills to do and they called for running two miles, I tried to run three. If we had to run it in 12 minutes, I tried to run it in 11. If I thought everybody was training for one hour, I thought I needed to train for an hour and a half.

That's called developing a work ethic. You need a good work ethic to move a mountain. Every chance to play in the backyard or in the driveway, to shoot tennis balls in the basement, to attend a practice, or to take a shift in a game is your chance to remove one more of the rocks it takes to move your personal mountain. If you don't take every chance or you goof off in practice or you come late or leave early, you are only cheating yourself. It's only your rocks that aren't being moved.

JAY

Let me tell you a story about Dan that will be a good example of his work ethic.

When he was just a freshman in high school Dan was a very good baseball player who led his school's team to a state championship. Although he never played the outfield before high school, he thought it was his best chance to win a starting position. After each regular baseball practice, we went to a baseball field near our home for additional practice. He would go into center field and I would hit fly balls to him—150–200 fly balls every night. While he stood in center field, I would hit balls to left field, then to right field. He would play in shallow center field and I would try to hit the fly balls over his head. He would position himself in deep center field and I would hit them short.

I would hit balls until my hands would begin to blister. I would beg to stop, and Dan would holler, "Just a couple more." He won that starting position in the outfield, and he played there for four years. He won All-City, All-Conference, All-District, and All-Regional honors. By the time he was a senior, he was named as one of the three best high school baseball outfielders in Michigan. And when he was a senior, we still went to that baseball field and did the fly ball thing. After he got to be the best, he worked hard to get better.

No one will or can move your rocks for you. Your parents, no matter how hard they may wish to try, can't get you to the NHL. They can't move your mountain or move even one of your rocks. They can sign you up with a better coach, send you to hockey camps all summer long, drive you to the rink at early morning hours, and buy you the very best equipment. All of this may make moving your rocks easier, but it is still up to you to move your mountain.

TRYOUTS ARE NEXT WEEK AND I'M SCARED I WON'T MAKE THE TEAM

12

> CONFIDENCE DOESN'T COME OUT OF NOWHERE. IT'S A RESULT OF
> SOMETHING . . . HOURS AND DAYS AND WEEKS AND YEARS
> OF CONSTANT WORK AND DEDICATION.
>
> —*ROGER STAUBACH*

DAN

Psychologists (people who study human behavior) tell us that we perform better if we are a little anxious about doing well. So being a little scared or anxious is a good thing.

I want to share a secret with you. Of the 50 or so guys that attend each NHL training camp every fall, three-fourths of the guys attending have exactly the same worries that you have about not making the team. I've had them every fall and I've gone to eight NHL camps. So you're not the only one.

How do you overcome the anxiety of not doing your best, of not being good enough, of failing? By becoming confident. Well, you might say, how do I change anxiety into confidence? One word—preparation.

Preparation means hard work and practice and then more hard work and more practice. For example, in school you know that you will be tested on the math material you are presently studying. You can pay attention in class, be diligent in completing your homework assignments, and perhaps do *all* the math problems even if your teacher only assigns the *even-numbered* ones. You can ask your teacher or parents questions if you are uncertain about some of the material. If you do that, you may still be anxious about the test, but you will be confident that you have done what you could to do your best on it.

The same is true if you are trying out for first chair in the trombone section of the school band. You know challenges are coming and you know the piece you will be tested on. You can practice it until you own it, until you and your trombone make the music the composer intended, until you can play it in your sleep. Again, you may still have some anxiety about being good enough, but you will have developed the confidence that you will do your best.

Suppose you've played for the A team in your hockey league and some of your teammates are going to try out for the AA team. Since you want to play at the highest level you can, or maybe just because you want to continue to play with your friends, you want to make the AA team, too. So you have to give yourself a chance to make it and the confidence that you can make it. Make sure you are in condition. Work on those parts of the game you need to improve. Skate or roller blade every chance you get. If you know part of the tryout is a one-mile run, you be ready to run the mile in the best time you can. Stick handle in your driveway with a tennis ball by the hour. You work hard, you practice a lot, and you get prepared.

What happens when you've actually done over and over again what you will be called on to do on the test or in the tryout? You come to believe, or have faith, that you can do it. That's what confidence means (*con* from Latin meaning "with" and *fides* meaning "faith"). This faith in yourself and your ability that comes from hard work and practice is confidence. You will feel it, others will see it in you, and then, often a wonderful thing happens: as a famous psychologist once said, "The confidence of success often brings actual success along with it." That is, if you believe you will be successful, often that will enable you to be successful.

The opposite is also true. If you haven't practiced enough to master the material, the music, or the game and you are not sure you can do it, doubt will lurk in the back of your mind as well as ride on your shoulder. And if you don't think you can do it, the people watching you will get the same message. A lack of confidence is hard to hide.

So if tryouts are in your future, and you're scared you aren't going to do well, now is the time to turn your anxiety into confidence by working hard and practicing hard. Roger Staubach was a famous quarterback for the Dallas

Cowboys. He once said, "Confidence doesn't come out of nowhere. It's a result of something . . . hours and days and weeks and years of constant work and dedication." Hard work and practice breeds confidence. Confidence breeds success.

JAY

Learning to overcome anxiety is one of the reasons Dan and I have such strong feelings about kids participating in amateur sports. On many levels, athletics provide examples of what life is like. Just like there are tryouts for the AA team, there are tryouts for entrance to college such as college entrance exams and your high school grade-point average. There are tryouts for the college team, tryouts for your first job, and tryouts for almost everything. Grownups just have different words for these tryouts. They call them interviews, talent searches, finding a mate, board exams, making a sales presentation to a big account, or running for office, to name just a few examples.

In each of these grownup tryouts there is a level of anxiety, just like you feel when you are trying out for the AA team. If you can learn that you can turn your anxiety into confidence by preparation, you will have a better chance to make the AA team and a better chance of being successful in all the types of tryouts in your life. It's yet another reason to play amateur sports—to learn important life lessons when you're young and before adult-type consequences follow adult-type failures.

Another important life lesson that can be learned in amateur sports is how to handle not making the team. Sometimes even when you've done your best, it isn't good enough or someone else is better. It's important to learn two things. If you didn't make the team, it doesn't mean you are a failure; it only means that your skills didn't measure up to that particular level or you were not the type of player that specific coach was looking for. And your abilities and the type of player you are depends on you. You can improve your skill level by working harder and practicing longer. The second thing to learn is that usually when one door closes on you, another window of opportunity opens.

This second lesson was often true for Dan in his career. When he didn't get to play in the power play, he developed into an outstanding penalty killer and that became his ticket to the NHL. He was cut from Winnipeg's AHL farm team (the Moncton Hawks), but went on to excel in the ECHL so that he got called back up to Moncton. That led to an NHL contract. If Dan had quit after any of his disappointments, he would probably be an accountant now. Instead, he worked hard and turned these disappointments into stepping-stones to the NHL.

One more thing about confidence: it's important to know the difference between being confident and being cocky. Cocky is thinking you can do it *without* the preparation. Confidence is thinking you can do it *because of* the preparation. Cocky is usually loud. Confidence is usually quiet. A cocky person is usually trying to convince himself as well as those around him. A confident person is convinced of himself. I've heard people say, "It ain't bragging if you can do it." It's been my experience that people who can do it don't brag about it; they let their actions speak for them.

13 WHAT IF MY PARENTS WON'T LET ME PLAY AAA TRAVEL HOCKEY?

DAN

If your parents won't let you play AAA Travel Hockey, I think you're in some very good company: my brothers and I. My father and mother wouldn't let any of us play any level of travel hockey until we were at least 14 years old. Did that hold us back? Absolutely, positively not. One of us made it to the NHL. Three of us played college hockey and the fourth one certainly could have, but chose to concentrate on his education instead.

When I was 13, I learned that two of my friends who were the best players from my house league were planning on playing hockey for the Grand Rapids Whaler AAA Major Midget team. I thought it might be a cool idea to play on the Whalers with them, even though it meant a

40-mile trip to the rink in Grand Rapids. But I was only 13, so I didn't think it was an option for me.

The next year I was invited to play for the Whalers. My parents weren't so sure. They argued that the other players were 16 years old; I was only 14. I argued in favor of joining my friends. If they were going to play in Grand Rapids, why couldn't I? I was the same caliber player. Playing more games against better teams seemed like a good thing. While Mom and Dad weren't certain of the value of this step, they allowed me to play for the Grand Rapids team.

Everything I anticipated turned out to be true. The number of games and the talent of the teams the Whalers played against forced me to advance my game to new levels. But my parents' concerns turned out to be well-founded in a way that they were wise enough to foresee but I wasn't. Traveling twice a week to practice in Grand Rapids (an hour drive each way) proved difficult for everybody. But it was playing two games after a tedious three-hour drive to Detroit and then three tiresome hours back every weekend that began to suck the fun out of hockey. Almost all our games were away games because the Detroit teams refused to come to Grand Rapids to play.

By the end of the season I wasn't sure I wanted to play hockey anymore—ever. Had I been the one who wanted to do this? Were my parents pushing me, pressuring me to do what they thought I should do? What I did know for sure is that I wanted baseball to start as soon as possible.

One year of travel hockey almost gave me a terminal case of hockey burnout.

Now I hear of travel teams that play 80 games and travel by car from Chicago to Detroit to Cleveland to Indianapolis and St. Louis. Kids play five or more games on a weekend. Now that I'm a parent, I'm not sure that is in the child's best interest.

This I am sure about: if the NHL made up that kind of a schedule for grown men whose job it is to play hockey and who make a lot of money playing hockey, the players would refuse to do it. I also know this for sure: my father would never have allowed me to play that kind of schedule and I would not allow it for my son either. No one should play that kind of travel hockey at *any* age.

JAY

There were a number of reasons why we didn't allow our kids to play travel hockey at an early age. One of the reasons was the cost involved. We simply couldn't afford to pay for four kids in travel hockey.

Also, we were only two parents with two cars. We couldn't arrange to deliver each of the kids to four separate games and practices. We also couldn't go to the games to watch four different kids playing on four different teams.

Also, I saw that sometimes the best kids didn't play travel hockey because their parents couldn't afford it. It was also true that some of the kids that played travel hockey did so, not because they were so good, but because their parents could afford it.

But I have to admit, we thought about letting our kids play travel hockey. We moved to Chicago where there was a hotbed of travel hockey and fierce competition among teams to get the best players. Before our move we heard of a tryout at the Southwest Ice Arena for an AAA Major Bantam Team. Our oldest son Scott was eligible but had no equipment in Illinois. Nevertheless, we dropped in to see what the talent was like and met the owner of the arena, Mr. Frank D'Cristina. When he learned we were from Michigan and that Scott "played some," he insisted Scott try out for this team. He rummaged around and found a pair of skates and some gloves.

As I watched from the stands, it was clear that Scott would be a very good, maybe the best player for this team. Mr. D'Cristina pulled us aside and told us what a great opportunity this would be for Scott. It was D'Cristina's goal to assemble a team that would win the National AAA Major Bantam championships. Former NHL player Lou Angotti would be the coach. The team would spend the Thanksgiving holidays in Pittsburgh and the Christmas holidays in Toronto. We were assured Scott could play a leading role in the team's success. This was a chance for Scott to play on a world-class team. It was the kind of opportunity most parents dream of for their children and it was being handed to Scott on a platter.

On the way home I asked Scott what he thought about playing on Mr. D'Cristina's team. "In the first place, spending every weekend on the road and spending Thanksgiving and Christmas away from my family has no appeal, and second, there were some irritating little jerks in that locker room who have no idea of how good they aren't. It would take something to have to put up with those turkeys for a whole season. If it's all the same to you, I'll pass [on this opportunity]. I'd just as soon play [in house leagues] with my friends on the weekends."

It was a time when my principles got pinched a bit. For a fleeting moment there was a temptation to push him in the direction of this opportunity. Should I allow him to pass up what I thought would be an opportunity of a lifetime?

Right after that I heard Sparky Anderson's advice on a call-in talk radio show. A concerned mother said her son was a "can't miss" for major league baseball. His coach was trying to get him to go to a summer baseball camp which she couldn't afford. "But Mr. Anderson," she said, "I'll beg, borrow, or steal the money because I don't want to stand in the way of my son making it to the major leagues."

Sparky Anderson just about came right through the car radio. "Madam!" he said. "You save your money! Your son will make it to Major Leagues in spite of what you do for him, not because of what you do for him."

Then I knew I shouldn't push Scott to play for Mr. D'Christina's team. I went home and said to the kids, "We're going to find a good house league program to play in." None of us have been sorry since.

So if your parents have good reasons not to let you play travel hockey, they may have the same good reasons I had, or maybe they have others. And you might still wind up in the NHL just like Dan did.

MY FRIEND'S TEAM PLAYS 80 GAMES A YEAR. ISN'T HE GOING TO PASS ME UP?

14

FOR EVERY PASS I CAUGHT IN A GAME, I CAUGHT
A THOUSAND IN PRACTICE.

—*DON HUTSON*

DAN

This is a good question and one that your parents wrestle with right along with you.

My experience is that whether or not your friend passes you is up to you, not your parents. Remember I said that when I was 13, two of my friends left the house leagues we played in and traveled 50 miles to another city to play on a travel team? I only played about 30 games that year; they played about 70.

Our relative schedules were as follows:

Monday: I played in the backyard for one hour after school and three hours after supper. They didn't play.

Tuesday: I played for four or five hours in the backyard. They traveled 50 miles for a one and one half-hour practice and 50 miles back.

Wednesday: I played for an hour in the backyard and had a game. They had a game (they played in my house league, too).

Thursday: same as Tuesday.

Friday: same as Monday

Saturday: I had a house league game and played for four to six hours on the backyard rink. They spent three hours traveling to Detroit and played a one and one-half hour game.

Sunday: I played for four to six hours on the backyard rink. They played a one and one-half hour game and spent three hours traveling back from Detroit.

For the week, I was on the ice for 30 to 35 hours. They were on the ice for 7 hours. To be fair, we only had our rink during January and February, while their travel schedule began in September and ended in April.

But did they pass me up? No. I joined them on that travel team the next year and led the team in scoring.

My point is that it is not the game time that is important to your development. It's practice time and, more importantly, personal practice time that improves your skill. Let me explain. In the NHL during a typical 60 minute game (if you take a regular shift), you have the puck on your stick for about 30 seconds. That's all. And you shoot the puck on the average two or three times. Kids usually don't play 60 minute stop-time games, but let's say they do. That would mean they have the puck on their stick for 30 seconds per game at all levels of play, all the way down to Mites.

Compare that to the rink in our backyard. When we played two-on-two for one hour, I had the puck on my stick for about eight minutes and shot the puck about 20 times. So, one hour of two-on-two in the backyard was the same as playing about 15 games in terms of "puck time." On a Saturday we played for five or six or more hours on the backyard rink. That was worth 35 or 40 games as far as actually handling the puck and shooting (puck time). The two-on-two games also gave me much bigger and better competition than the travel league.

And an hour or two by myself or with my brother Greg (the goalie) was worth—well, it was priceless. Priceless because I think it was this quality practice time that got me to Juniors, to college, to the professional ranks, and finally to the NHL. Priceless also because my brother became my best friend.

So you want to keep up with your friend who's playing travel hockey? Roller blade for an hour with your stick and a street hockey ball for every game your friend plays. Shoot tennis balls for an hour. Or go to pickup hockey where the other players are bigger than you and at a time when it's likely there will only be 8 or 10 of you. These are the kinds of things that make you a better player, not necessarily a lot of travel games.

If your goal is to play college hockey, the most games you can play are 34 games. Those are the rules set down by the NCAA (National Collegiate Athletic Association) for young adults whose primary job is to get an education. But I think the colleges have it right. They practice four days to get ready for two games on the weekend. Eight hours of practice to play two one hour games. They, too, believe that it's not the amount of games that will improve you, it's the amount of quality practice time.

The Europeans also believe in a very high number of practices to number of games played. They practice three or four times for every game they play. Typically, they don't start playing games until they are nine. Before that, it's only practicing the skills necessary to play the game. We all know how successful their programs have been in sending players to the NHL with very high skill levels. Most of the leading scorers in the NHL are European players.

JAY

When my children were growing up, I heard a lot of people giving reasons why Canada produced so many more NHLers than the United States. The reason I heard most to explain the difference was "Canadian kids get more ice time." It followed, then, that if we wanted to get more of our kids into the NHL, they had to play more games. And it wasn't uncommon to hear of nine- and ten-year-olds playing on travel teams that played 80 games.

When Dan went to Canada, I had a chance to see the Canadian hockey system first hand. The first thing I learned was that the reason the United States doesn't have more players in the NHL is because kids in the United States have several sports to choose from. Some of our kids choose football, some choose baseball, and there's basketball, tennis, or golf as well as hockey. The talent pool in the United States is spread over four major sports and several minor ones. In Canada there is only one major sport. The talent pool plays hockey.

To watch Dan play basketball, I had to get to his Canadian high school in time for the seventh period of the school day. That's when the varsity basketball games were played. There were no other parents present and only a few students who were willing to skip a seventh-period study hall to watch the game. There was no Friday evening hoopla in a 2,000-seat gym packed with screaming students, parents, cheerleaders, and a pep band.

But on Friday night 2,000 screaming fans would pack the municipal ice arena to watch the town's Junior B team play the team from a neighboring town.

So in Canada if you want to be a jock, you play hockey. It's the country's game—almost a religion.

The other reason so many Canadians are better hockey players is that, in fact, they do get more ice time. But it's not the kind of ice time we imagine. It's ice time on the village outdoor rink or at the frozen pond at the quarry where pickup games begin shortly after school and last until the lights go out. It's the kind of ice time Dan got in our backyard.

In more recent years, the number of AAA games and summer tournaments have increased in Canada, which might lead to the conclusion that Canada is now producing more NHL players. In fact, the opposite is happening. Canada's proportion of players in the NHL in the 1999–2000 season was 56 percent, the lowest it has ever been.

I don't think it's possible to make the NBA without having a basketball net in your yard. That's why we did the hard work it took to make a rink in our backyard every year. I believe that rink was responsible for three of my four sons playing college hockey. The son who didn't play could have but chose to concentrate on his studies instead.

If you are concerned about getting enough ice time, be sure it's quality ice time. And while playing house or travel games is important, it may not be the quality ice time you need to develop your skills.

WHAT IF SPRING HOCKEY LEAGUES INTERFERE 15 WITH BASEBALL?

[MY DAD] WOULD HIDE MY SKATES. HE WANTED ME TO PLAY OTHER SPORTS, TO JUST BE A REGULAR KID HAVING A GREAT SUMMER. HOCKEY WAS THE FOCAL POINT, BUT IT WAS WHAT I DID IN THE WINTER.

—*WAYNE GRETZKY*

DAN

Play baseball. Play all the sports, not just the one you happen to like or are good at for the moment.

There are several reasons why I think this is important advice. At your age you don't know what sports you will really like or be good at a few years from now, especially if you don't try them. Scottie Pippen, for example, didn't play high school basketball. And of all the kids who played in the Little League World Championship Game throughout its history, only 21 went on to play in the Major Leagues, but 5 went on to play other professional sports—three in the NHL and two in the NFL.

In addition, all sports have skills that carry over to other sports. You can learn a lot about playing your position in hockey by playing baseball, a game where playing your position is just as important as in hockey. If you want to be a goalie in hockey, playing catcher in baseball is good training. The game strategies for basketball, hockey, and soccer are very much the same.

Soccer is a very good conditioning sport for hockey when there is no ice to be found. The footwork necessary for dribbling a soccer ball also carries over into being able to handle the puck with your feet. A lot of hockey players are good golfers because the hand-eye coordination and the hip turn are similar for shooting the puck and hitting a golf ball.

My parents encouraged my brothers and sister and me to play many sports, so I played basketball in junior high and high school, baseball every summer, and soccer in junior high. We played a lot of family tennis and I started playing golf when I was three years old. I still play on the church softball team with my dad and brothers, and because of my baseball experience, I can still hit a dinger from time to time. Because of my golfing experience, I am invited to appear at a lot of charity golfing events and I usually don't embarrass myself.

I don't think it's wise to play just one sport at age eight or ten. You ought to be having fun with sports and learning about all of them. If you told your parents you wanted to be a doctor, they wouldn't suddenly enroll you just in medical courses. I think it's just as silly to play only one sport when you are young.

So play all the sports you can. They will help you become a better athlete, and (listen to me about this) *it's the best athletes who make it to play professional sports.*

JAY

Dan is not the only NHLer who played other sports. At least five NHL players played in the Little League World Series including Chris Drury, Ray Ferraro, Stephane Matteau, Yanic Perreault, and Pierre Turgeon. Brendan Shanahan and Joey Nieuwendyk were great lacrosse players. These NHL players obviously did not just play hockey.

There are other NHLers and their parents who would have the same advice as we do. Scott Frasier of the Rangers indicated he didn't play summer hockey until he was 17. "Kids should play soccer and baseball and tennis. You don't need to play [hockey] 12 months of the year." And the father of Don Sweeney of the Bruins says, "I don't believe in 12-month sports and I'll say that flat out. If you read the autobiographies of a lot of the great athletes, you'll see they played many different sports."

I think one of the most important reasons why you should take a break from hockey or any sport you're concentrating on is to avoid getting sick of it. If you are playing 50 or 60 games a year, you have time left for school and little else. It doesn't matter how much you like the sport; there is a good chance you'll tire of it, and it will no longer be fun.

Because Dan played all sports, by the time hockey season rolled around he hadn't been skating for about six months. So he couldn't wait for his first game and hardly slept the night before. He was also sad to see the season end. That's a lot different than some kids I've seen who, after 50 games and two or three summer hockey camps, can hardly stand to lace up the skates and get into that smelly gear one more time.

Dan talked earlier about making it to the NHL as being like moving a mountain with your hands. If removing the rocks from the hockey mountain is no longer fun, you'll move on to a different mountain or forget about moving mountains all together.

16 | I LIKE PLAYING FORWARD, BUT MY COACH WANTS ME TO PLAY DEFENSE. WHAT SHOULD I DO?

IT IS ALWAYS PLEASANT TO BE URGED TO DO SOMETHING
ON THE GROUND THAT ONE CAN DO IT WELL.

—GEORGE SANTAYANA

DAN

There are two good reasons why you should do as your coach asks and play as a defenseman or at least give it a try. The first reason is the same reason my father used to give me when I asked why I had to do something he'd asked me to do. He would say, "The best reason you have is because I told you to do it." What he meant was that as a parent, he had a lot more experience than I did and knew better than I did what was best for me. Given that, I should respect his experience and wisdom and do what I was told. Your coach is older and more experienced than you and it's his responsibility to decide what's best for the team. You respect him as your coach, so the best reason you should do as your coach asks is because he asks you.

There are other reasons to do as you're asked. At your age either you are playing hockey to have fun or to develop into a better player. If you're only playing hockey to have fun, you should play where you're going to have the most fun. You may want to continue to play forward, but how do you know for sure that's where you'll have the most fun if you haven't tried the other position?

If your goal is to develop into a better player, you should do as your coach asks for these reasons:

- Learning how to play the defensive position will make you a better forward later on if you decide you would rather be a forward. You see, if you play defense for a while, you will learn how defensemen have to turn, have to think, and what skating maneuvers are more difficult than others. If you learn how a defenseman thinks, this knowledge should help you be a better forward if and when you change back to that position. It's like learning the enemy's secrets.

- If you are a forward and play the position well, there will be times when you have to cover the point if a defenseman rushes the puck or gets caught out of position. There will also be times when you will be called upon to defend against a rushing player. If you know something about the moves that are required of a defenseman and are able to make those defensive plays when called upon, you will be a better player and be more valuable to your team. You will be a better "two-way player." That means you know what to do when your team has the puck, but you also know what's required when the other team has the puck.

🏒 You don't know now at your age, what position you will wind up playing when you are older. Let me explain. My college roommate, Ken Klee, is a good defenseman for the Washington Capitals. But there have been times when the Caps had too many good defensemen and not enough forwards. Ken was asked to step up and play some games as a forward. Because he had played as a forward in youth hockey, he was able to step in and play that role. His ability to play both positions saved his job with the Caps and most likely lengthened his career in the NHL.

My former teammate, Steve McKenna, came up through college and the pros as a defenseman. He now plays forward. There wasn't any room for Steve as a defenseman as the Kings had a very solid core of blue-liners. But Steve was able to prolong his stay in the NHL because he could make the switch from defenseman to forward.

As for myself, I shoot left but I play right wing. That's because my college coach came to me and said that the team had too many left wingers, would I be willing to play on the right side. I respected the coach (and knew if I played on the right side I would get more ice time) and agreed to try to play on the right side. I found out I preferred playing on the right side, something I wouldn't have known if I didn't try it. Now, because I was willing to follow my college coach's suggestion, I can play either side. That gives my coaches in the NHL, some flexibility with me that they don't have with some other players and that increases my value to the team.

🏒 Perhaps the coach sees something about you that you don't see for yourself. It may be your size or your speed or your sense of the game. A good example of that is Jay Riemersma, who grew up not far from my hometown and now plays tight end for the Buffalo Bills. He was an outstanding high school quarterback and went to the University of Michigan on a football scholarship to play quarterback. But Michigan had several great quarterbacks and the coaches at Michigan thought that with his size and his knowledge of the game, Jay would make a great tight end. Jay agreed to convert to tight end and became outstanding at that position. He was drafted by the Bills and he just signed a new four-year contract for a lot of money. Left to his own ambitions, Jay Riemersma would have remained a second string quarterback in college and he would have never played in the NFL if he hadn't been willing to listen to and respect the judgment of his coaches.

For these reasons, I advise you to give playing other positions a try. At the very least, when your team does one-on-one drills, do the drill as a defenseman if you are a forward or as a forward if you are regularly a defenseman. It will make you a better player; you may find out you like the new position better than the old one; and you may be better at the new position than you were when you were at the old. It just may be the thing that prolongs your career or helps get you to the next level, and you may help the team out in the process.

17 HOW MUCH OFF-ICE TRAINING SHOULD I DO?

A BARBELL NEVER SCORED A GOAL.

—DAN'S TEAMMATES ON THE
LOS ANGELES KINGS

DAN

It may surprise you to learn that I didn't know anything about off-ice training until I got to college. During the summer before my freshman year, I received a training manual from the coaching staff of BGSU that outlined what I should be doing before I got to school. Before that, some of the guys on my Junior B team and I messed around with weights, but nothing serious. Before college, my off-ice training consisted of playing baseball and golf in the summer and soccer in the fall.

Now I hear of PeeWees and Major Bantams being required to do weight training. I think that weight training is serious business. And things that are serious should be left to adults. Training for kids should be about fun—so weight training does not come with a strong recommendation from me. And because weight training is serious business, I think it makes you more serious about the sport than you should be. Before high school, hockey should be about having fun and developing your skills, not your muscles and your physique.

Having said that, I know of no scientific data indicating that weight training, done correctly, is bad for you. The key here is "done correctly," meaning done under the supervision of a qualified weight trainer. Russians and Europeans who compete in the sport of weight lifting, typically spend a whole year just learning how to train without weights before they start lifting. This time is spent learning the proper technique and speed.

Equally important, I was told by the professional weight coaches at the L.A. Kings (who have a worldwide reputation) that weight training for kids may improve their coordination and skeletal structure but does not significantly increase strength. A more direct benefit from weight training only occurs after a person's skeletal and muscular structure has matured (after reaching puberty). Testosterone, a hormone that is necessary to build muscles, is not generated by your body until you reach puberty. Weight training done *after puberty* and done properly with supervision from a professional strength or weightlifting coach will establish correct form and will build sport specific muscles.

So while weight training won't damage you (if done correctly and under close supervision), it won't give you significant benefits until you are 13 or 14 years old. Weight training before that is not necessary, it's not all that beneficial, and you have other things to be doing like schoolwork and other sports that will benefit you much more than doing reps on a weight bench.

You may wish to do exercises in which you resist the weight of your own body, like sit-ups and push-ups. So if you are obsessive about doing weight training, do those exercises that use the resistance of your own body, under the supervision of a professional. And if someone scoffs at doing sit-ups, for example, in favor of bench presses, know that every NHL camp I've attended included sit-ups as part of the fitness test (they stop you at 120).

Another kind of off-ice training is also for conditioning. For adults, about the only way to get that kind of training is running. I'm not as opposed to young kids running to stay in condition as I am to weight training. But there's no need to run for running's sake. You would receive more benefits from playing baseball, soccer, or basketball. Not only do you get exercise and conditioning by playing the game, but you'll develop other athletic and strategy skills that will carry over to hockey. Two obvious examples are learning to handle the puck with your feet through soccer and give-and-goes and picks in basketball. Playing catcher in baseball is great off-ice training for hockey goalies. In basketball, the ball is bigger than a puck and the basket is smaller than a hockey net, but the game is played with two forwards, a center, and two guards (defensemen) and the strategy is very similar. It's true that they don't allow goal tending in basketball and they throw the ball up for a jump ball instead of dropping the puck like in a face-off, but those differences are only because basketball hasn't developed as a sport to the point that hockey has!

The players in the NHL are all outstanding athletes, but I know of no one among them who is a world-class weight lifter or a great runner. I think you are much better served by developing your athletic skills, your coordination, and your competitive skills by playing other sports than by weight training and hockey-specific conditioning.

Besides, other sports can be a lot of fun; you meet other kids, and who knows whether or not there is another Michael Jordan or Mark McGwire hiding inside of a Bantam hockey player somewhere. At one time Chris Drury, the hockey player, was hiding inside a Little League Baseball Championship pitcher.

All of this is not to say that if you are having a problem with some aspect of your game that you shouldn't work on that problem. If you have a problem with quickness—like I do—there are drills you can do off the ice to improve that. If you are having a problem with stickhandling or catching a pass, by all means get a street puck or a tennis ball and work on that in your spare time. But you don't need to be doing bench presses or running two miles a day at age 10 to make it to the NHL.

18 WHAT IF MY COACH OR MY PARENTS THINK YOU GUYS ARE FULL OF BUNK?

TOO BAD THAT ALL THE PEOPLE WHO REALLY KNOW HOW TO RUN THE COUNTRY ARE BUSY DRIVING TAXICABS AND CUTTING HAIR.

—*GEORGE BURNS*

DAN

You should continue to respect your parents and coaches and do as they say because they're your parents and coaches.

There are a lot of people in youth hockey who have different ideas about what it takes to succeed in hockey, whatever succeeding means to them. A lot of folks do not agree with my father and me about what it takes to succeed. In this book we tell you about what we think is important: to get good grades, to play hockey to have fun, and to play all the sports to develop into a good athlete. We think that skill improvement comes from individual practice and playing against bigger, better, faster players and not necessarily from playing 80 or more games a year when you are 11 years old.

Most coaches and managers in youth hockey have quite a different view as to how to "make it." They emphasize playing a lot of games and learning complicated game strategies. I was once told by a coach that his Squirt team played more than 80 games, had an 80-page playbook, and skated the "left wing lock." I was a little embarrassed because I had just finished playing in the first round of the Stanley Cup playoffs and the Kings' playbook only had four pages. I didn't know what to say. After I had these Squirts in a hockey clinic, however, I learned they couldn't make or catch a pass and wondered how much fun a player had playing 80 games without the ability to catch a pass.

So I wouldn't be surprised if your coach or your parents scoffed at what they might consider my father's and my homespun ideas. After all, who are Dan Bylsma and his father? Up until now, the only reason I could ask you to believe a word I say is because I made it to the NHL, and some of your coaches and your parents didn't play hockey, let alone college or professional hockey, and very few if any of the players who ever played for your coach or in your city's program ever played college hockey or made it to the NHL.

But something is happening in Canada that everyone— players, parents, coaches, and general managers—should be aware of. It's called "Open Ice" and it's a discussion going on in the highest levels of youth hockey in Canada. You see, the Canadians are concerned that their national sport is being taken away from them. As we stated earlier, the percentage of Canadians in the NHL in the 1999–2000 season was only 56 percent, the lowest it has ever been. And most of the Canadians are second- or third-line players. With a few exceptions, the top talent now comes from countries other than Canada (and it's not the United States). Canadian teams no longer dominate the Olympics and the World Cup. In the 2000 NHL All-Star game, the World team beat the North Americans (Canadians and United States born players) 9–4.

At the 1998 Olympics in Nagano, the Czech Republic, which has one-nineteenth of Canada's numbers in youth hockey participation, won the gold medal. Finland, with one-twelfth Canada's numbers, knocked off Canada in the bronze medal game. The record of the United States as a producer of skilled players in the NHL is equally as dismal.

Many Canadian youth hockey leaders are saying that the quality of Canadian hockey players has declined because their kids play too many games, do not practice enough, no longer play on the frozen ponds where individual skills are learned and improved, and concentrate too much on hockey and don't play other sports which is necessary to develop into good athletes. These leaders deplore the teaching of defensive systems, teaching of and using body checking instead of skating and puck handling, and coaching to win instead of to develop. The people who are saying these things are people like Ken Dryden, Bobby Hull, Mike Bossy, Glen Sather, Réjean Houle, Frank

Mahovlich, Howie Meeker, Bruce Hood (former NHL referee), and Derek Holmes (former head of Hockey Canada).[1]

So the things we've been telling you are supported by people in Canada who have been very important in hockey, both amateur and professional. If USA Hockey begins to seriously wonder why there are not more U.S. players among the top players in the NHL and why the USA National teams do not do well in competition with teams from other countries, they will come to the same realization that the leaders of hockey in Canada are coming to now. When that happens, you can say you heard it here first.

---

[1]Much of the information in this chapter is taken from a 12-part series beginning on April 4, 1998, entitled "A Game in Crisis," by William Houston, a sports reporter for the *Toronto Globe and Mail*. The article was republished in its entirety in the December 22, 1999, issue. It can be obtained at *http://globeandmail.com/series/hockey/gameincrisis/*.

19 | *I NEED BETTER SKATES!*

I COMPLAINED ABOUT THE LACK OF SHOES
UNTIL I SAW A BOY WITH NO FEET.

—AUTHOR UNKNOWN

DAN

If you look closely at the picture of me on the cover of *So Your Son Wants to Play in the NHL,* you will see that I am wearing a pair of Lange skates. These were my brother Jon's skates before they were mine, and they were my oldest brother Scott's before they were Jon's. And believe me, they were not top-of-the-line, custom-fitted skates when Scott got them new. With four boys playing hockey and one of them a goalie, my parents had a tight budget to keep us in sticks. In fact, my father used to go to the broken stick barrel and fish out sticks that could be reglued and repaired for us to use on the backyard rink.

From the time I could skate, there were few birthday or Christmas gifts that were not clothes or hockey gear. You were really happy to see an older brother get a really good pair of gloves because you knew that in a few years they would be yours. I never lacked for adequate equipment, mind you, but I rarely got anything new, and it was never the most expensive or the best until I got to college.

There was a family in our hockey program that always outfitted their kids with the latest equipment. It almost made you want to puke because the kids didn't appreciate what they had, didn't know what it was worth, and treated it carelessly. You got the impression that they thought they couldn't play well unless they had the very best and latest equipment. The fact was that they couldn't play well even with their superior equipment. But they looked good in the team picture.

The point is that equipment doesn't make the player, just like expensive uniforms don't make a team. My dad tells the story of taking a team made up of house players from our city to play a travel team from a nearby city. The house players had matching jerseys, but that was all. All of the players had different socks and some had a different colored sock on each leg.

The other team had matching everything, including equipment bags and parent's jackets. But the mismatched homeboys thumped the matching boys each time they played. That didn't seem fair to the travel team. They had spent more money on equipment and looked better for the team picture, but the winner is decided by how many times the puck goes into the opposing net, not how good the players look for the team picture.

It may be hard to imagine, but I made it to the NHL largely on hand-me-down equipment. A lot of my teammates in the NHL come from working class families and they are no strangers to used equipment either. Matter of fact, most of us don't use new equipment now. Most of us like to break in a pair of shoulder pads or shin guards and wear them until they fall apart.

JAY

If any of my children ever came to me and said, "I need new skates," we would have a discussion about the difference between needs and wants. We would agree that a need is something you cannot get along without. A want is something you would like to have but don't need. For example: you needed food; you wanted prime rib. You needed to do your homework; you wanted to play hockey on the backyard rink.

Dan's mother and I agreed to provide all of our children's needs and half of their wants. If they needed skates, we would provide adequate skates. If they wanted better skates, they had to pay the difference between what they needed and what they wanted.

Usually they ended up with what they needed, not what they wanted.

If you are used to getting everything you want, this may seem like cruel and unusual punishment, but our children learned two very important lessons. The first was the value of equipment. If adequate skates cost $200 and the skates they wanted cost $300, they learned the value of a dollar because it took a lot of hours of mowing lawns or picking blueberries to make $100. Most often, they figured out that they couldn't skate $100 worth better in the more expensive skates. Also, they learned that it wasn't worth 30 hours of mowing lawns at $3 an hour to get the more expensive skates. The second lesson they learned was how important it was to take care of the equipment they did have because they knew it was not easily replaced.

There's another reason why you may not get new skates or the best skates. Hockey is a very expensive sport. I know of no parents who support their children's goal to play hockey who do not give up things they might want for themselves so their child can play. Perhaps your parents need every spare dollar they can come up with so you can play. Some moms need to work out of the home so that their children can do extra things, like playing hockey. I knew a dad who worked overtime to make the extra money it took for his kids to play hockey. These things take precious time out of parents' lives so you can have the privilege of playing.

I don't know how to tell you what it costs to play hockey in terms you can understand, but I'll try. A homeless person could buy a 99¢ Whopper for supper every night for 12 years for what it costs for you to play travel hockey for one season. Your parents could buy thirteen new television sets, or take a second honeymoon to the south of France, or have lovely dinners at fancy restaurants every Saturday night for two years for the same cost of one kid playing travel hockey for one season.

So if your parents say, "We can't afford the $100 extra to buy the top-of-the-line skates you *want*," maybe they're thinking about how many Whoppers they *need* to buy. Maybe they're thinking about a night or two on the town for themselves, and if they are already paying for you to play hockey, maybe they deserve it.

WHAT'S IMPORTANT TO LOOK FOR IN A SUMMER HOCKEY CAMP?

20

PEOPLE RARELY SUCCEED UNLESS THEY ARE HAVING FUN
AT WHAT THEY ARE DOING.

—*DALE CARNEGIE*

DAN

I've been to a few summer camps, I've worked at a lot of summer camps, and I've held my own summer camps for quite a few years, so I know something about how they work. The first thing to remember about summer hockey camps is that it's a want, not a need. We talked about the difference between a want and a need in the last chapter.

Why go to a summer hockey camp at all? The main reason why you might benefit from going to a summer camp is because the programs in your area might have volunteer coaches like my father. He's a great guy, but he's no Larry Robinson, one of my coaches with the L.A. Kings and a member of the Hockey Hall of Fame (sorry, Dad). He couldn't help me improve my skating except to tell me I had to be faster. That told me what I needed to do, but not how to do it. Going to a good summer hockey camp can be like going to the doctor to find out what's wrong with you (in this case, your skating) and make you better.

There are three things to look for if and when you and your parents choose a summer camp. I list them in what I think is the order of importance:

1. Does the camp say in their brochures that you will have fun? That is important because hockey is a game. Games are supposed to be fun; summer is for fun. If summer hockey camp is not fun for you, you will quickly grow to dislike it, you won't work at what the instructors are telling you, and you will be wasting your time and your parents money (and your money, too, if you've worked to help pay for the camp).

2. Are the instructors good teachers? That is important because besides going to summer hockey camp to have fun, you go to learn. I might be the best hockey player in the world, but if I can't share what I know with you, my secrets are locked up in me. For example, the instructors need to understand the mechanics of skating and be able to explain and demonstrate (we'll call that *tell and show*) what these mechanics are. And their tell and show must be done in such a way that you can understand what they are telling you and can then tell your body what it has to do to

skate like they're showing you. That takes a very good teacher.

3. Does the brochure say that the camp stresses learning how to skate properly? That is, does it teach skating fundamentals? Why is that important? Everyone knows how to skate, right? I've had more than 750 kids and adults come to my camps, and they all could learn to skate better, most of them a lot better. In a typical game you spend almost all of your playing time skating. But you stickhandle for only about 30 seconds. Maybe you shoot the puck four or five times, and you check someone three or four times. Does that give you an idea of the importance of learning how to skate correctly? Besides, if you can skate better, you most likely will have the puck on your stick more, shoot more, and check and avoid being checked better. If you can't skate, you can't play the game. The game is skating.

Those are the important things to look for: fun, good teachers, skating. There are other things that may make the summer camp experience more enjoyable: a video analysis of your stride which will allow you to see what you look like compared to a professional skater; good off-ice instruction like plyometrics; assurances that the big-name stars in the brochure are actually there for the whole week on the ice with you; nice ice rinks; a place to do off-ice activities if it rains. But these things are icing on the cake if you can have fun, be exposed to good teachers, and learn to skate better.

JAY

I have two things to add to what Dan says about summer hockey camps. But first, what's this about I'm no Larry Robinson? A *good* son would let his father think he was the best coach that son ever had!

Seriously, the first thing I'd add to what Dan said is that hockey camp will be more fun and you will probably learn more if it comes after you haven't skated for a while. When Dan and his brothers were young, their season ended in April, so they hadn't skated for four or five months when the hockey camps were in late July or August. They looked forward to camp so much there was no need to worry that they wouldn't give the camp their best effort. If they had been playing in the winter, had been in spring leagues, and then added a summer league to their schedules, I'm afraid the camp would have become ho-hum, a yawner.

I favored summer camps that were sponsored by and run by college or university coaches. There were three reasons for this choice:

1. I thought that the coaches connected to a college would likely be good teachers.

2. I thought they would be able to give me an idea of my children's potential and progress at their age.

3. I wanted my children to have a taste of what college was about. I wanted them to see the buildings, walk on the campus, and experience what going to college would be like. It was part of a plot to steer Dan and his brothers toward going to college when they got old enough.

So if you are undecided, you will probably not go wrong if you enroll in a summer hockey school run by a college coach. There are also some good nationally known camps that hold sessions in nearly every part of the country, like Planet Hockey Skill Camps. Also Robby Glantz runs very good skating clinics all over North America.

As he told you, Dan runs a summer hockey camp. It is not affiliated with a college. But all of Dan's instructors are chosen because of their proven ability as professional hockey players. In addition, they are all college graduates, fun to be with, good teachers, and each of them is with the kids the entire camp, on or off the ice.

Dan practices what he preaches: kids have a lot of fun, there are good teachers, and they teach skating fundamentals. There's one other thing Dan didn't mention, but what you may learn from reading this book: he's a very good role model (except when he says that I'm no Larry Robinson).

21 IF ONLY I COULD PLAY ON THE POWER PLAY!

DO YOU KNOW WHAT MY FAVORITE PART OF THE GAME IS?
THE OPPORTUNITY TO PLAY.

—*MIKE SINGLETARY*

DAN

When I was in Juniors many of my teammates would say, "If only I could get a chance to play college, then I could really shine. My game is more suited to the college game." When I got to college, many of my teammates were looking forward to the opportunity to play professional. That was where they were sure they would shine. Next I played in the East Coast Hockey League where players would do anything to get just one game in the I (the International Hockey League or IHL) or the A (the American Hockey League or AHL). When I played in the A and then in the I, players were sure that if they would only get a chance to play in "The Show," they could *really* show what they could do. Then, when I finally made it to the NHL, there were players who were sure they would do much better if they played on a different line or for a different coach or for a different team.

What most of these players failed to realize is that whenever or wherever they stepped onto the ice, that *was* their chance to shine. Whenever or wherever you play or practice, you have an opportunity to show what you can do. You never know when someone is watching who has the ability to give you your next break or next opportunity.

Every time you step on the ice or onto the court is an opportunity to be seized or squandered. Whether you play on the power play, kill penalties, or play center or wing is not as important to your future success as how hard you work at whatever position you play or situation you're in.

I truly believe if I had tried to make it to the NHL on my scoring ability, I'd be an accountant now. My point is that if one opportunity is taken away from you, seize another. Or work harder to regain the position you want, whether it's being the quarterback or playing on the power play. Remember that if you don't play on the power play, you will most likely play on the very next shift. You can seize that opportunity or squander it. Squandering an opportunity may lead to the temptation to make excuses. Excuses are crutches to help you feel better, but it's hard to play hockey on crutches.

JAY

In the beginning of Dan's sophomore season in college, he was a scoring machine. After six games he led the team in scoring. He was among the top scorers in the CCHA, and he was making the highlight films.

Then his coach decided to move him from the second line (a scoring line) to the third line (a checking line) to "beef up that line." Dan went from scoring a goal a game to scoring one goal every six or seven games. And he never got a chance to play on the power play.

Although Dan was not happy about being moved to the third line, he didn't whine or sulk. Instead he figured out that if he wanted to get noticed, there was an opportunity on the penalty-killing unit. It was not as glamorous as the power play or the second line, but it was an opportunity. He worked very hard at it and became one of the best penalty killers and shot blockers in the CCHA. He once scored when his team was down 3 on 5!

Dan's skill at penalty killing got him noticed by pro scouts and was probably his ticket to the NHL. He most likely wouldn't have made it on his offensive skills. So he turned a roadblock (not playing on the power play) into a ramp, a ramp that took him to the NHL.

Dan is right. Every time you step on the ice, you have an opportunity you can seize or squander, and you never know who may be watching.

22 | *WHAT IF MY COACH DOESN'T LIKE ME?*

DAN

When we are growing up, life outside of what is familiar
to us can sometimes be scary. It might be anything from
a trip to the store by yourself for the first time to going to
the city library. And that certainly includes playing for a
new team or a new coach. New things are often scary
when we're kids because we haven't matured and we're
not as full of confidence as we might be when we're older
or when the new becomes familiar. We also want to be
liked. We want to be appreciated. And we don't know if
we will be liked or appreciated when we are involved in a
new situation.

Having been to an NHL training camp or two, I can tell
you that some of those feelings never go away, even when

you're a grown-up. So if I had those feelings in an NHL training camp, feelings of new experiences being scary and wanting to be liked and appreciated are normal when you're a kid.

In most cases our fears of not being liked or appreciated go away when we grow accustomed to the situation. But sometimes these feeling don't go away, and we begin to feel that the coach doesn't like us or appreciate us. We don't get enough ice time or we don't get on the power play. At those times we rarely look to ourselves. Instead we blame the coach. We feel or say, "The coach doesn't like me."

I've played for a lot of coaches on a lot of different teams in the past 20 years. They range all the way from coaches who didn't know a lick about hockey and didn't own skates to a coach who is in the Hockey Hall of Fame and has almost as many Stanley Cup rings as he has fingers. All of the good coaches had two things in common: they liked to work with and help kids and young adults, and they liked to win.

These two characteristics usually work in your favor. You need help and you like to win. So the relationship between you and your coach is usually based on common goals. I'm not saying that all coaches are good coaches. Nor am I saying that it's easy to get along with all coaches. But based on common goals, it should be a good relationship. If it's not, the first place to look is to yourself. If this is not the first coach who you thought didn't like you, look really hard at yourself. Perhaps you're not doing the things that every coach likes, or perhaps you are doing some of the things your present coach doesn't like.

What are some of the things every coach likes? You can put hard work on the top of your list. And the list will also contain things like these:

- working hard when you practice
- working hard when you play
- being courteous by being on time, telling him in advance if you cannot be at a game or practice, listening when he speaks
- being respectful of him, the officials, your teammates, and equipment, both yours and theirs
- being coachable by doing what he asks you, following his game plan, taking suggestions as to how you can improve
- being in control by not taking retaliating penalties, coming off the ice promptly when a line change is made on the fly, watching your temper and your language
- being helpful by cleaning up your share of the tape balls after practice and taking your turn at being water boy or picking up the pucks after practice
- being selfless by passing the puck to a teammate on a 2-on-0 with an open net, welcoming new players to the team, correcting the score sheet if you are credited with an assist that belongs to someone else

- being ready to play by having all your equipment, being sure your skates are sharpened, and having enough tape

You can put all of the things on this list into a simple rule: work very hard, play very hard, and be a gentleman or lady (girls play hockey, too) in the process. Do these things and chances are the coach will like and appreciate you and the contribution you make to the team. Most likely, you will stand out from the me-first attitudes that are so common in sports these days, and that will not go unnoticed by the coach.

What are some of the things that coaches don't like? Put being lazy at the top of the list. My dad used to address lazy play by saying, "I don't hear any music playing!" What we knew he meant was that we were playing hockey, not going to a public skate session where one can leisurely skate to waltz music. The rest of the list would include these:

- being discourteous by missing practice or a game without warning or explanation or by coming late
- being disrespectful by talking back to the coach, mocking a teammate or opponent, mouthing off to the officials, or using foul language
- not accepting coaching by following your own game plan instead of the coach's, or whining when things don't go the way you think they should go

- being undisciplined by being a puck hog, staying out a little or a lot longer after the lines have changed (and cutting into the next guy's shift), taking bad penalties, or not being in control of your temper or your tongue
- being a slob by not cleaning up after yourself
- being unprepared by never having enough tape, needing to get your skates sharpened 10 minutes before game time, or forgetting some of your equipment

You can put all of the things on this list into a simple rule, too: be a lazy, inconsiderate jerk. The reason coaches dislike the behavior in this second list is because it goes against the reason they coach in the first place: to help kids and to win. Kids who do the things on the second list usually don't want any help and this kind of behavior often prevents the team from winning. Further, having one inconsiderate player on a team can take away the fun for others.

It may be possible that you have all the good characteristics on the first list and your coach still doesn't like you or appreciate you. There are some coaches whose behavior we can find on the second list. But I believe those are the rare exceptions. And the good thing about it is you will only have to play for them for one or two years, and you shouldn't make it an excuse for holding up your career.

But if the coach really doesn't like you, and particularly if this is the second coach who doesn't like you, it may be because you do some of the things on the second list. If that's even partially true, I'm not sure you are someone I'd like to coach or play with either.

JAY

What Dan has said shows he understands productive and destructive behavior very well. Of course he speaks from a lot of experience. What he has not said is that his work habits, his courtesy, respect, and willingness to do what he is told to do helped him make it to the NHL. Here's an example of what I mean.

When Dan was playing in the ECHL, his coach was Jeff Brubaker. Dan's goal was to get promoted out of the ECHL into a team in the A (American Hockey League). On any given day, a coach from a team in the A might need a player to replace one who was injured. He would call Coach Brubaker and say, "We need a forward. Could you recommend someone who could help us out?"

At that moment Coach Brubaker has the fate of all the forwards on his team in his hands. Someone from his team is going to get a big chance and

Brubaker has to decide who it will be. How will he make that decision?

Brubaker will make it so that he will look good. Why? Because he wants the selection to reflect well on himself. He wouldn't mind getting promoted to coach in the NHL, so he's going to pick a player who will be a credit to his program. He will pick someone who is a hard worker, who will be coachable, a player who will be in control.

And who comes to mind? Well, Dan Bylsma came to his mind several times. Dan consciously worked at having those characteristics mentioned in his first list. If Dan were lazy, loud-mouthed, inconsiderate, uncoachable, or a whiner, Brubaker would be sending him down a league, not up a league. Coaches recommend the good guys for promotion—the guys who will be a credit to their program. They get rid of the undesirable ones.

Jeff Brubaker later told me what he saw in Dan. He said, "It was immediately apparent when Dan came to us that he was a quality person. We were surprised that someone of this caliber had filtered down to the ECHL. The fact that he was a million miles from the NHL did not seem to lead him into the rut that most players in this league get into, consumed by the feeling that they had too far to go to make it. Dan seemed to operate on the theory that if he did everything possible to become the best player he could be, someone would notice and he would get a break. He was right."

Notice Coach Brubaker didn't say Dan was talented or tough. He said Dan was "a quality person" and that he was a high-caliber person and that he "did everything possible to become the best player he could be." He was talking about characteristics from Dan's first list. So being a quality person is as important as being a good hockey player. It made Coach Brubaker, like every other coach Dan has had, like him.

Dan has seen both productive and destructive behavior and understands the consequences of each very well. That's why I think he will make a very good coach himself some day.

23 | *DO I HAVE TO HAVE* THAT *KID ON MY LINE?*

MANY A MAN WHO THINKS HE'S TOO BIG FOR THE LITTLE JOB
TURNS OUT TO BE TOO LITTLE FOR THE BIG JOB.

—AUTHOR UNKNOWN

DAN

Every team has a worst player. Every team. If you make a list of everyone on your team and rank them in order of ability, someone will be at the bottom of the list. And if the worst player quits, or gets traded, someone else will become the worst player. You'll still have a worst player. I played on a team once that had two worst players. Neither of them quit or was traded, either. Sometimes the worst player is really bad, and we all know who *that* kid is.

My first "*that* kid" experience happened when I was a PeeWee. A family had a son who had never skated before, but his parents decided that it would be good for him to learn to play hockey. And, as luck would have it, we got him on our team. The league's rules dictated we had to play him in a regular shift like everyone else. My dad put him on a line with my friend Tommy Ferguson and me.

My older brother Jon played on that team as well as several other very good players. My dad had three lines to choose from. He could have put him on either of the other two lines. But, no, as my luck would have it, my dad put him on a line with Tommy and me.

I asked my dad, "Do we have to have *that* kid on our line?"

My dad kidded me at first. He said, "Every one wants to play with you, Danny. This kid's just luckier than the rest." But then, "Listen, all we have to do is teach the kid offsides and you and Tommy can carry the line by yourselves. And besides, do you remember when you were the worst kid on the team? It's not a good feeling. I expect you to treat him like you would like to be treated." Then he kidded me some more saying, "Sit next to the kid on the bench. Maybe some of you will rub off onto him!"

I wasn't sure I had anything of myself to spare, but Tommy and I took the kid under our wing, which must have looked funny because the kid was three years older and about six inches taller than I was. I think it took four or five weeks before the kid understood what offside was. So his not being able to skate was not our biggest problem. For those weeks Tommy and I had to skate like the wind to beat him over the blue line to prevent offsides.

Did the inexperienced kid hold us up? Plenty of times. Did he go offsides often? For the first few games, every chance he got. In the grand scheme of things, did it harm me to have to play with him? No. As a matter of fact, that was the same year we won the championship and Tommy Ferguson got all those goals.

My dad's instructions to *that* kid were, "Wait for Tommy or Danny to carry or shoot the puck over the blue line, then go for the net with your stick on the ice." It was good advice for *"that* kid," and it's not bad advice for anyone.

Did *"that* kid" have a good time? He had a wonderful time and even banged in a few rebounds himself standing by the net with his stick on the ice. And his stick in the air when he did manage to score brought pandemonium (that's shouts of joy and high fives) from the rest of the guys on our bench.

I have another "Do I have to have *that* kid on my line" story to tell you. It was at my very first L.A. Kings training camp. I had just gotten in line to see the eye doctor when the door opened and in came Wayne Gretzky. He exchanged niceties with some of the players waiting in line in front of me as I stared in awe. When he got to me, he stuck out his hand and said, "Hi, I'm Wayne Gretzky."

If there was some cool reply to be made, I couldn't think of it. All my tongue could manage was to blurt out something that only faintly resembled "I'm Dan Bylsma." The Great One, the man who didn't need any introduction, had introduced himself to me! What he didn't say, and what he could have said is, "Do I have to play on a line with *this* guy?"

Later, when I got my first game in the NHL, Larry Robinson sent me out to play on the power play with Gretzky and Jari Kurri. Here was the best player and one of the best players ever to play professional hockey. And Dan Bylsma. Remember Tommy and I and *that* kid? This time I was *that* kid, except by that time I knew what offside was!

I will always be grateful that Gretzky and Kurri didn't say "Do we have to have *that* kid on our line?" They may have thought it, but they were kind enough, professional enough, and gentlemen enough not to say it. And I will never ask "Do I have to play with *that* kid on my line?" again. Ever.

JAY

Two true stories. And there's an important lesson to be learned from those stories. There is no game so important that it gives us the right to be hurtful or cruel to another person—especially to another who is less fortunate, less talented, less experienced, or perhaps hasn't had the opportunities that we have had. I can be accused of nagging my children on this point; I've said it hundreds of times, "Never dump on anyone."

Why? There are three reasons that come quickly to mind:

1. Because there's no one so good that he cannot play with someone of lesser ability. As Dan says, "If Wayne Gretzky could play with me, you can play with anyone."

2. Because your moral compass should point toward being kind, not cruel, toward being helpful, not whining. Because you're never too young to begin to be a gentleman, and one definition of a gentleman is one who never makes another feel uncomfortable.

3. For a selfish reason. Because the toes you step on today may be connected to the backside you have to kiss tomorrow.

Three good reasons to "Do onto others as you would have them do unto you." That may include playing on a line with *that* kid.

24 BUT IT ISN'T FAIR!

DON'T CRY OVER SPILLED MILK.

—ENGLISH PROVERB

DAN

Every time one of my brothers or I would complain that something wasn't fair, my father would say, "You're right, it wasn't fair. But life isn't fair." I used to hate that answer. I wanted justice. I wanted him to set things right.

Now I know something about life not being fair. At first it was little things. For example, I remember being called out at the plate when the umpire said I didn't touch third base when I was rounding the bag. Instead of winning, we lost. I *had* touched third base. My father (who was coaching at third base) saw me touch third base. The home plate umpire was in no position to see if I touched the base. But he called me out, anyway. It wasn't fair.

My father used the occasion to say one more time, "It wasn't fair. But life isn't fair."

When I was 16 years old, I was selected to attend the Michigan Select Midget Camp. From this camp players would be selected to attend the USA Hockey Select Midget Camp. I was playing Juniors in Canada while nearly all the other players at the camp had only played Midgets. The General Manager of my Juniors team told me that Central Scouting had ranked me in the top 20 of all 16-year-olds in Canada and the United States. This camp would be selecting the top 20 of the 16-year-olds in Michigan.

I led the Camp in scoring, but I wasn't selected to go to the USA Hockey Select Midget Camp. I was hurt, I was angry, and perhaps even bitter. It wasn't fair. But by now I knew the answer to "It's not fair."

During my sophomore year in college, I was leading the team in goal scoring. I got removed from a scoring line to a checking line. I thought I had proved that I should be on a scoring line and on the power play. I didn't think it was fair.

On January 15, 1998, our little baby girl died two weeks before she was to be born. I know something about what's not fair. Life's not fair.

You have two choices when things happen in life that aren't fair. You can use it as an excuse to give up on fairness and life. Or you can recognize it as a fact of life and go on about the business of being fair yourself and living your life to the fullest.

I didn't go to the USA Hockey Select Midget Camp, but I went back to Canada and was one of the leading scorers in the Western Ontario Junior B League. I received something a lot of guys at the Michigan Select Midget Camp didn't get: a college scholarship.

I didn't get to be a big scorer in college, but playing on the penalty killing unit and being a defensive forward forced me to develop a skill that got me to the NHL. None of my classmates made it to the NHL even though they played on the power play, were the top scorers, and made the CCHA All-Star teams.

We lost our baby daughter, but now we have a son, Bryan Thomas, who was born January 3, 1999, and is the joy of our life.

Life isn't fair. But how you react to unfair situations will largely determine how you are affected. Life isn't fair. But life can be good if you choose to make it that way.

JAY

In everyone's life, things happen that aren't fair. Bad things happen to good people. That's because the world's not perfect (yet). There are bad calls, there are bad breaks, there are bad people who seem to get away with bad behavior. There are bad diseases, and there are untimely accidents and deaths. It's part of being human.

But just as being human includes the possibility for things that aren't fair, it also includes the possibility for great happiness, joy, love, accomplishment, and peace. And these good things are all the more wonderful when contrasted to the things that aren't fair. When I told my children that "Life's not fair," I meant, "You're right, but dry your tears, wipe your nose, and get on with life. Don't cry over spilled milk. Don't look back at what isn't fair, look ahead at the possibilities that remain for you."

Dan is right, and he speaks from some very painful experiences. But you, like he, can either give up on fairness and life, or you can make the best out of what is left. Dan's life is a good example of choosing the latter. All the way to the NHL.

25 | WE LOST, BUT IT WASN'T MY FAULT!

THE GREATEST OF FAULTS IS TO BE CONSCIOUS OF NONE.

—*THOMAS CARLYLE*

DAN

You may have noticed that some of the last few chapters were about excuses.

> *"I need better skates."*
> *"If only I could play on the power play."*
> *"The coach doesn't like me."*
> *"Do I have to have* that *kid on my line?"*
> *"But it isn't fair!"*

Perhaps you didn't think of these chapters that way, but that's what they were about. Now I'd like to talk about an excuse that will be more damaging to your career than all of the excuses listed above; that is the claim "It's not my fault."

"It's not my fault" is the most damaging of all excuses because it allows you to think you're not responsible for the outcome of your shift on the ice or the outcome of the game. Further, "It's not my fault" may affect the outcome of your career and ultimately the outcome of your life. It tricks you into thinking that someone else is responsible for your failure. "It's not my fault" allows for the possibility that your team's loss, your lack of skill, your lack of progress, your not knowing the rules, your poor grades, your not being able to get along with other people—all of these things are someone else's doing.

Is it possible that none of these things were your fault? But when your team wins, if you raise your level of skill, if you know the rules, if you get good grades, and if you can get along with other people—are all of these things also someone else's fault?

Perhaps you can see the point I'm trying to make. You can see how easy it is to give excuses for your failures and take credit for your successes. Believe me when I tell you that your chances of making it to the NHL or any other success in life will increase if you take responsibility for your failures and give other people credit for your successes.

I mean, really, whose fault it is that you didn't score? Is it really because you need better skates? If that were true, everyone in the NHL would be scoring machines. We all have the very best skates, any brand we want, custom fitted. You didn't score because of you, not because of anyone or anything else.

The same is true in school or anything else in life. You didn't get a bad grade because you needed a better pencil or your textbook wasn't new. We all need to take responsibility for our own actions.

One of my teammates in youth hockey was not skating well because his skates were very dull. My father was our coach and he asked the kid what was the matter. The kid said, "It's not my fault. My skates are dull, I don't have an edge."

My father quickly replied, "That's okay, I'll take the blame."

The player looked at the coach with puzzlement. "It's not *your* fault."

My father said, "But you said it wasn't *your* fault. You aren't willing to take the responsibility for your skates, and I'm responsible for this team, so it must be my fault."

The player made sure his skates had a good edge from then on.

I find myself coming back to the example of moving your own mountain. Whether it's the NHL or any other goal you set for yourself, it's your mountain to move, one rock at a time. Saying "It's not my fault the rocks aren't getting moved" leaves the mountain just as tall, with just as many rocks remaining to be moved as before you said "It's not my fault." But overcoming the problem or correcting the fault is a process that removes one of the rocks on your path to success.

So rather than dismissing your failures with the biggest excuse of all, "It's not my fault," take responsibility. Because you *do* have responsibility. You have the ability to correct and to respond to your failures. Let's call it *response ability*. And that response can be "What can I do to make the situation better?" It can be "How do I use this setback to my advantage?" It can be "What can I learn from this failure?" It can be "What can I do to be sure this doesn't happen again?"

Or it can be "It's not my fault." That response won't get you to the NHL. Most likely it will only get you to the next excuse.

The "It's not my fault" excuse is not limited to amateur hockey. It's been known to find its way to the NHL as well. Sometimes when things are not going well—for example, maybe I haven't scored in a while or my team is not doing as well as everyone would like—it is easiest to look at everyone else for the reasons. My linemates, the goalie, or the coach can become easy targets. And I have to remind myself to look in my own mirror. I need to ask myself, "What can I do to make things better? Do I have to work harder? Do I need a better attitude? How can I make the situation better?" I can say "It's not my fault," but most likely I share the blame because I'm a member of the team.

Remember the team of mismatched players that my brother played on that beat the travel team with the matching everything? There was something else about that mismatched team that few people knew. One of the forwards, a good forward whose name was Chris, did have a legitimate excuse. Chris had only one leg. Because of a birth defect, his left leg ended just below his knee. He wore a prosthesis (a mechanical leg). Having a wooden leg could have been an excuse we would have all accepted. He could have said, "I can't play hockey, I only have one leg and it's not my fault."

But Chris wanted to play hockey. He became so good that no one could tell he only had one leg. Can you possibly imagine how hard he had to work to become a good skater? Chris had all the excuses I mentioned here. He could have said:

"I need better legs."
"I could play on the power play if I had two good legs."
"The coach doesn't like me because I only have one leg."
"It's not fair that I was born like this."
"It's not my fault that I only have one leg."

And the other kids on the team could have said, "Do we have to have *that* kid on our line?"

And we all would have understood. But Chris was a person who decided not to be handicapped by his handicap. He worked hard and developed into a very good player. In fact, he still is a valuable member of a men's league team he plays on. I include Chris's story to honor a young man who chose not to use any excuses. Instead his determination and spirit inspire everyone who knows him and his secret. I'm honored that Chris thinks enough of me to send his son to my hockey camp each year.

So tell me, what's not your fault? What's your excuse? And as I said before, excuses are crutches that may help you feel better, but it's hard to play hockey with crutches.

JAY

I'd like to expand just a bit on what Dan said about you taking responsibility for yourself. It's *not* your parent's responsibility to get you to the NHL. In fact, they can't get you there. That's true no matter how hard they may want it for you, or how bad you want it for yourself. Not their money, their prayers (and I believe in prayer), or all their hopes and dreams will get you there. It has to come from you. It's not their job. And if you don't realize your dream, it's not their fault.

As Dan has said, it's your rocks that have to be moved and only you can move them. At the very most, all your parents can do is make it easier for you. They may be willing to drive you to the rink instead of you having to find your own way. They may help build a rink in your backyard. They may be willing to hit fly balls to you as I did for Dan. Even if they give you everything they can, they can only open the door for you. You have to walk through the door. That applies to school, sports, music, art, whatever your goal is. Your life and the individual aspects of it are your responsibility. If you don't accept that responsibility, you may say, "It's not my fault," but it *is* your fault.

After Dan got to the pros, he often called home after a game to tell us how he had done. I remember one such call when he had done very well. I said, "So how did you do?"

"We lost 5–4."

"But how did you do?" I asked.

"Two goals and two assists."

I said, "That's outstanding!"

"But we lost."

In other words, two goals and two assists wasn't enough. The team still lost. Dan still took responsibility for the loss. It *was* his fault; he didn't do enough to get the win. No excuses. If you haven't done what it takes, you haven't done enough, and you bear some of the responsibility.

SOMETIMES MY PARENTS ARE LOUD/CRITICAL/ PUSHY! HOW CAN I HANDLE THAT

26 RESPECTFULLY?

EVERYONE HAS A PURPOSE IN LIFE, EVEN IF IT'S ONLY
TO SERVE AS A BAD EXAMPLE.

—*AUTHOR UNKNOWN*

DAN

I don't have much personal experience with loud/critical/pushy parents because I was lucky enough to have two parents who were quiet (my father rarely said anything during a game if he was a spectator), very affirming, and only asked that I do my best—and did so in private and never scolded or berated me in public. But I've seen a lot of other parents whose behavior at games would have embarrassed me if I were their kid. It's not a pretty sight.

One thing I do know: loud/critical/pushy parents (and sometimes their loud/ critical/pushy children) show up at NHL games and behave like loud/critical/pushy fans. That's not a pretty sight either.

Because I don't have a lot of experience with problem parents, I'll let you read what my father has to say about it.

JAY

It's important to be sure hockey is a sport that you want to play. If you want to play basketball, it only takes a $20 ball and the playground down the street and for 10 kids in sneakers to have at it. If you decide to play hockey, it takes a lot of parental involvement and commitment. That's where loud/critical/pushy can come in. There's the up-front money—$500 minimum for *used* equipment before you take the ice. And the time—rinks are not located in every neighborhood. Then there's the ongoing expense of ice time, sticks, tape, etc. So when your parents have invested this time and money for you to play, if you don't try to do your best or if you lose interest, they might be justified in being upset with you. So be sure hockey is something you really want to do and will stick with because it requires a lot of money and commitment on the part of your parents as well as you.

If you have loud/critical/pushy parents (let's call them Elsie Peas—short for LCPPs—loud/critical/pushy parents), the most important thing you can do is remember how much you dislike their conduct so that when you are an adult and your kids are playing, you don't become an Elsie Pea. That may solve the problem for your kids, but what about you?

Remember that Elsie Peas behave that way because they love you and care about you. They want you to be successful and to have good experiences, not bad. Their intentions are good, but they haven't learned how to convey those intentions in a healthy way. And in the excitement of the game, sometimes even adults forget their manners and their good intentions and engage in behavior they would regret if they saw themselves on instant replay. Your understanding this behavior may make it easier to accept, but it doesn't change the behavior. What can you do to make a difference?

If you have a coach who is as sensitive to your parents' behavior as you are, you could ask him to speak to your parents to remind them that "Attaboy" is good, but yelling "You stupid idiot" is a no-no. If it appears the official made a mistake, "Every one makes an occasional mistake" is good, but screaming "Don't quit your day job, you dummy" is a no-no. One coach I know held a parent-versus-son scrimmage game at the beginning of the season. Of course a team of even average Squirts can beat moms and dads who haven't skated. After the game he would say to the parents, "Before you're critical of your child's play, remember that the kids beat you out there tonight and I would rather have them on my team than you." He made humble folks out of would-be Elsie Peas.

If your coach is also an Elsie Pea, that's an additional burden to bear and I'm sorry for you. In that case, you may have to be the adult by saying something to your Elsie Peas. If they are loud and yell bad things at the game, you might say something like. "It's not helpful to the team when the fans are abusive. It sets a bad example." Notice there's no "I" or "You" in that statement. To say something like "I hate it when you scream and holler at me" may be taken as disrespectful and not have the result you hope for. Saying something like that points the finger directly at and scolds the Elsie Pea. Not many parents enjoy being scolded by their own parents let alone their children. By saying "It's not helpful to the team when fans are abusive" and "It sets a bad example" you are not judging their behavior. Rather, you are appealing to their good nature and asking them to be a benefit to the team. Most parents would respond positively to that kind of a comment and some might even realize their conduct has been out of line.

If your Elsie Peas are critical, you might try saying things like "I'm trying to do the best I can, sometimes I make mistakes," or "The game's not fun if you get mad." Or you might say "Dad, it's a game, I do this for fun. I don't think I'm going to make my living playing hockey." Remember, to be respectful. If you sass back at your parents, they will be angrier at you for that than they were for your missing the empty net.

If you are being pushed to play the game after you no longer enjoy it or would like to try something else, the time to decide you want to give it up is not in the middle of the season. I can guarantee you will hear things like "You made a commitment to the team" and "You're the only goalie the team has. What is Coach Smith going to do? He can't find another goalie now" and "You can't quit now, we have too much money tied up in equipment." If you want to quit the game and you think your parents will resist (perhaps because the NHL is their goal for you and not your goal for yourself), do it well before the season starts. Then there is no commitment to the team and the team isn't relying on you.

Also, have a good alternative in mind. For example, you might try saying "I don't think I will have the time for hockey next season; my teacher has asked me to compete in the science fair competition at school." Or "What would you think of us spending the money we would otherwise spend on hockey on my taking private trombone lessons instead." Or "I don't think I will have the time to do both junior high football and basketball and hockey next year and I think I'd like to try my hand at fullback." Substituting another admirable activity for hockey will likely be acceptable with your parents. And there may be a side benefit. Elsie Peas are not as noticeable at band concerts or science fairs as at hockey games.

So remember how Elsie Peas behave and don't behave like that when you have children. Also, remember usually Elsie Peas get carried away because they care for you and want the best for you. Try to get your coach to speak to Elsie Peas who are not acting responsibly, and if you do need to be the one to talk to your Elsie Peas, do it respectfully and in a non-judgmental way. If you want to quit the game, do it at the end of the season or before the season starts. Your Elsie Peas might find your quitting easier to understand and accept if you have a worthwhile alternative.

WHY SHOULD I LISTEN TO MY PARENTS? THEY'RE NOT THAT SMART!

27

> THOSE WHO CANNOT REMEMBER THE PAST
> ARE CONDEMNED TO REPEAT IT.
>
> —*GEORGE SANTAYANA*

DAN

When you are a baby, you can't make any decisions for yourself and your parents make all the decisions. When you're young, your parents make a lot of decisions for you. As you grow older, you begin to make more decisions and they make fewer. About the time you turn into a teenager, your knowledge and experience grows so quickly that it seems you don't need your parents very much, if at all. In fact, often the decisions they make or try to make seem stupid. For the life of you, you can't understand why they can't see the obvious answers to questions that you see so clearly.

If you think about it, some of the decisions your parents made for you when you were about five years old were to your benefit. They decided, for example, not to let you play in the street. Because you are still alive to be reading these words, you can understand that was a good decision. They also decided that you should go to school. Because you are able to read these words, you can agree it was another good decision on their part.

Although your parents were smart enough to make those good decisions when you were five, sometimes it seems they are out of touch with what's cool today. They insist on decisions and behavior that is strange, even stupid from your perspective. I know. I've questioned a decision or two that my coauthor made from time to time when I was your age.

I've learned something about decision making since then. I learned that you can make a decision by analysis and/or by experience. For example, a little child who is approached by a well-dressed, nice-looking, well-spoken person who offers candy could analyze the situation. Well-dressed is good. Nice looking is good. Well-spoken is good. Candy is good. I don't see anything bad here. I'll go for the candy.

You can analyze the situation even better than the little child can, but you have the advantage of experience. Everything may appear good, but you know from experience that things are often not as they appear. Strangers don't give away valuable things without a motive, and you have heard that this is a way strangers kidnap children.

You will come to a different decision than the inexperienced little child.

In the same way your parents' experience leads them to their decisions as to what is best for you. It's experience you don't have yet. And for as smart as you think you are now, your parents were that smart 30 years ago.

So you can ignore their advice or you can use this 60 years of experience (30 years' worth for each of them) as a vast resource to help you. And if your parents are like mine, they will welcome the chance to help. After all, they've been helping in a big way since you were born.

"Mom, what would you do in this situation?" will do more than get her advice. It will make you feel very much like your family is a valuable support system for you. And to tell you the truth, I still call my mother and my father for advice. I ask them about my NHL contract, about the house I'd like to buy, about how to raise my little son.

Why? They still have 60 more years experience than I do.

JAY

The things Dan said about how valuable a resource your parents can be for you is also true about coaches and teachers. It becomes obvious if you think about why we have coaches. We need somebody to make decisions about who will play with who, when the lines are changed in hockey, or who bats in what order in baseball.

Actually, in a perfect world, we wouldn't need a coach, the team members could decide among themselves. But we don't have a perfect world and we can all imagine the bickering and fighting that would go on in deciding a batting order or line changes if it were left to the players.

So we have a coach and we choose an adult for that job. But why do we have an adult? We could elect a team captain and give him the responsibility for the batting order or the lines and line changes. But from experience, we know that that wouldn't work very often. We choose an adult because an adult has the experience to make the decisions, know the rules, and teach us something about the game. Often former high school or college players coach. Your parents might try to get you on their team. Why? Because of their experience.

A philosopher named George Santayana once said, "Those who cannot remember the past are condemned to repeat it." You can't remember a lot of "past" because you don't have a lot of "past." Your parents, your teachers, and your coaches have experienced a lot more "past" (life) than you have. That includes experiencing mistakes as well as successes.

You can borrow from the great wealth of their experience at no cost. In doing so you may be spared the grief of repeating their mistakes and making a lot of your own—at great cost.

Ignoring or rebelling against this great wealth of experience and accumulated wisdom may have serious and undesirable results.

28 WHAT'S WRONG WITH SNEAKING A BEER?

ALCOHOL IS A LOT LIKE IGNORANCE: THE MORE YOU HAVE OF IT,
THE LESS YOU ARE ABLE TO SEE ITS EFFECT ON YOU.

—JAY

DAN

I have *never* known a situation in which the use of alcohol, drugs, or inhalants helped anyone anywhere—in athletics, in school, in music, or with friends. I *have* seen the use of alcohol, drugs, or inhalants limit a person's ability to function athletically and cause him to act stupid socially, do poorly in school, and be unsafe behind the wheel. I have also seen individuals who were bigger, stronger, and more talented than I ruin their hockey or other sports careers by the abuse of these illegal substances.

Given all that, don't do it. Besides, it's against the law and the advice of your parents, and we just talked about the value of that advice.

I know. I know. Nothing bad will happen to *you*. *You* can handle it. *You* are smarter than the kids who misuse it. *Your body* won't react negatively. *You* know when to say "enough." *You* are not influenced by peer pressure.

Right.

But *you* have a mountain to move. And having a mountain to move, you need all the clarity and presence of mind you can get. The mountain can't be fuzzy, in psychedelic colors, or floating. And you don't need some stupid act, done under the influence of alcohol or drugs, to cause you to have your mountain taken away from you before you get a chance to move all of it.

You are the reason not to get involved with alcohol or drugs. Don't lose all your potential for a cold drink or a short buzz.

JAY

I know that a lot of underage kids drink and do dope. All too often I read newspaper accounts of teenagers who die in auto accidents in which alcohol is one of the contributing factors. I don't believe for a minute that only the kids who get in fatal car crashes drink. I also had five children go through junior high and high school and have chaperoned my share of dances and had to call the parents of kids who had seriously abused alcohol and couldn't find their way home safely.

I'm also aware that my kids did not totally abstain from drinking when they were underage. I'm grateful I caught them before the police did, or before I had to pick them up from a highway accident with a sponge.

As Dan said, alcohol and drugs can't help you get to the NHL but could harm you and/or cause a lot of problems with your parents, your school, and the law. With those kinds of odds against it, why do kids still get involved with substance abuse? I think it's because of ignorance. Alcohol is a lot like ignorance: the more you have of it, the less you are able to see its effect on you. Think about that.

HOW DO YOU GET ATHLETIC SCHOLARSHIPS FOR COLLEGE HOCKEY?

29

WHAT'S ONE OF THE MOST IMPORTANT THINGS YOU CAN DO TO MAKE IT TO THE NHL? GET GOOD GRADES IN SCHOOL!

—DAN

DAN

You can start getting ready to be recruited for an athletic scholarship now, no matter how young you are. How? By getting the best grades in school you can as we discussed in Chapter 4 because athletic scholarships are only given out to players with good grades.

I want to start by saying the procedure for getting an athletic scholarship is the same for girls as it is for guys except it's easier for girls because there are fewer girls playing hockey for the number of scholarships available for girls than for guys. So you go, girl!

Guys or girls, the thing you need is to be noticed. A college coach or recruiter needs to know about you and see you play. How does that happen?

There are two ways to be noticed. One way to be noticed is to play hockey where the college coaches regularly come to watch for and scout prospective recruits. So where do college coaches scout?

- Junior A and some Junior B teams in the United States and Junior B and Tier II Junior A teams in Canada are the main places colleges look for talent. Junior teams are for players who are 16 to 19 years old. There are presently more than 35 Junior A teams in the U.S. and about the same number of Junior B teams and many more Junior B and Tier II Junior A teams in Canada. These teams are the highest level of competition you can play and still be considered eligible to play college hockey. Tier I or Major Junior A teams in Canada are considered semiprofessional and if you are associated with (either try out for or play for) a Major Junior A team, you become ineligible for college hockey.
- Prep schools that have good hockey programs and high schools in some states like Minnesota and Massachusetts where there are outstanding high school hockey programs are also scouted.
- Select camps run by USA Hockey.

College coaches regularly visit these teams and Select camps and establish relationships with their coaching staffs and general managers. If you are a good player and indicate you want to play for the Bowling Green State University (BGSU or BG), for example, the general manager or the coach will call Buddy Powers, the coach of BG and suggest BG come and scout you.

You may be wondering how to go about playing for a Junior A or Junior B team. Most of these teams have websites that list the coach, tell a little of the history of the team, and sometimes indicate how many of their players went on to college or to the pros. These sites also show when and where tryouts are held in the fall. To get a tryout, have your current coach write a letter of recommendation so you get an invitation. These teams also scout for players just like colleges do. So on the recommendation of your coach they may scout you or ask for tapes of your games.

Am I saying that if you don't or can't play for any of these teams you can't get recruited? No way. So what do you do if you don't have a Junior team in your area, you can't go to Canada to play, your high school doesn't have quality high school hockey, or you can't afford to go to a prep school?

In your junior year of high school, have a tape made of your best games. Send the tape along with a letter expressing an interest in playing for all the schools you would consider attending. This package should also include a history of the teams you've played for, your statistics, your GPA (here's where the good grades come in) and college entrance exam test scores, and a schedule of when and where you will be playing in the foreseeable future. You should also ask your current coach for a letter of recommendation in a sealed envelope to send along. Of course, if he can say that you're certain to be the next Cammi Granato if you are a girl or the next Jaromir Jagr if you are a boy, your tape would go into the college coach's VCR immediately. I am aware that this sounds like a long shot, but coaches get a number of these kinds of packages each year and they take them seriously.

JAY

It is important to plan how you are going to pursue a spot on a college hockey team. As Dan said, the good grades part should start in whatever grade you're in now. Assuming you don't go to a prep school or a high school that gets scouted by college coaches, you should be thinking about where you want to play and when. It might be best to set a goal for when you want to enter college and work back from there.

For example, if you want to play college right after Grade 12, then you should be planning to play Major Midgets in Grade 10, Junior B in Grade 11 and Junior A in Grade 12. If you are already behind that schedule, that is you are still playing PeeWee or Junior Varsity in Grade 10 and you know you won't be able to play Junior A or B in Grade 11, you can push the schedule back one year by planning to play Junior B in Grade 12 and Junior A the first year out of high school while attending a junior college for one year.

The key here is to have a plan and begin to plan early. Ask your current coach what you need to do to elevate your game to the next level so that when the tryouts for the next level comes, you have been working on the skills you need to make that team and play at that level.

It also doesn't hurt to try out for a team even though you may not be ready to play at that level. For example, if you are going into Grade 11 and you plan to play for a Junior A team in Grade 12, try to get invited for a tryout for the Junior A team now (again, your current coach should be a resource for you). That way the Junior A coach will see what you can do, will tell you what you need to work on to make the team next year, and you will see the skill level of the present Junior A players. Then next year, the tryout procedure will not be new to you, the coach will be looking for you, and he will be familiar to you and you to him. He will be impressed if you made noticeable improvements in the areas he suggested, and you will have a better chance to make the team than if you walked in off the street cold and unknown.

30 WHAT ARE YOU GOING TO DO WHEN TIME RUNS OUT AT YOUR LAST GAME?

THIS IS THE WAY THE WORLD ENDS. / THIS IS THE WAY THE WORLD ENDS. / THIS IS THE WAY THE WORLD ENDS; / NOT WITH A BANG BUT A WHIMPER.

—*T. S. ELIOT*

JAY

Throughout this book, Dan and I have been talking about what it takes to make it to the NHL. We've talked about how much you have to want it, what your chances are, how hard you have to work for it, and what kind of character it takes to make it.

For just a moment, I'd like you to think about life after hockey, whether your last game comes when you're a Bantam, a high school player, or even an NHL player. For most of you, life after hockey will come sooner rather than later. But even if it comes later and you do make it to the NHL, you will still have more than half of your life to live.

In Chapter 4 we talked about how important it is to get good grades because (at least in the United States) colleges and universities are the farm system for nearly all professional sports. You need good grades to get into college, and very good grades to get into the best colleges. We also talked about the wonderful opportunity you have to get knowledge and dispel ignorance, to learn about great ideas, great literature, art and music, and the sciences.

There is another reason to get a good education. It will help you live a quality life after hockey. There will be jobs to do, communities to live in, votes to cast, families to raise, and perhaps youth hockey teams to coach. As you go about preparing yourself for the NHL, you must also be preparing yourself for life.

Hockey may not end for you because you didn't try hard enough or weren't good enough. Sometimes it ends because of an injury on or off the ice, through no fault of your own. Sometimes it ends because of a health problem that doesn't allow you to play.

For all these reasons, it is as important to work on your education, to have balance in your life between sports and education, sports and the arts, and hockey and other sports as it is to work on your hockey. Yes, you might benefit from going to a good hockey camp in the summer, but also take piano lessons, go to Space Camp, read a great book, and watch the Discovery Channel as well as "Hockey Night in the NHL."

We encourage these things because we want your life during and after hockey to be a rich and rewarding one whether you make it to the NHL or not.

31 WHAT ABOUT FIGHTING IN HOCKEY?

> TO SURVIVE IT IS OFTEN NECESSARY TO FIGHT AND
> TO FIGHT YOU HAVE TO DIRTY YOURSELF.
>
> —*GEORGE ORWELL*

DAN

We think there is absolutely no place in youth hockey for fighting or a coach that condones it or a parent who thinks it's cute or macho. Period. None of my brothers or I *ever* fought in youth hockey because my father made it very clear that we wouldn't get to serve any fighting penalties because he would be over the boards to take us off the ice himself (and we thought he meant it).

Fighting is within the rules of *professional* hockey. And I'm going to talk about fighting in *professional* hockey.

Hockey is a very fast game that is meant to be played with a high level of intensity. This intensity sometimes results in tempers flaring. Some players are known for being hacky and wacky, especially when the ref's not looking. Even a peace-loving kind of guy like me can put up with only so many whacks in the back of the legs and cross checks to the back of the neck. Sometimes you have to stand up for yourself or a teammate and you are unavoidably involved in a donnybrook.

I've often played on a line with Ian Laperriere as my centerman. "Lappy" plays hard and has been known to deliver a solid check or two during his career. He also isn't afraid to tell an opponent that he's such a loser that he couldn't even win first prize in his team's "Ugliest Player" contest. So when Bob Probert (a left winger) lined up to take a face-off against Lappy late in the third period in a game against the Blackhawks, I knew it wasn't because Chicago thought he could win the draw. Nor did they think that Probert would take the puck end to end, score, and tie the game.

While Lappy can usually hold his own, he's forty pounds lighter and five inches shorter than and no match for Bob Probert. So I had a decision to make. Do I act dumb and let Probert have at Lappy, or do I step between them and probably save Lappy's life while risking my own?

I risked my own, and fortunately Probert didn't want me, he wanted Lappy so I wound up dancing with Jim Cummins. Tussles with two of the NHL's toughest guys in the same shift. Fortunately they both were as tired at that point in the game as I was and they didn't hurt themselves or me. But it was a time in a game where I had to step up for my linemate and myself.

I know of no one in professional hockey who enjoys fighting or who sits in the locker room before the game and says "Tonight I hope I get into it with so-and-so." Every enforcer and mucker I know would rather be known as a 40-goal scorer.

But the reality is, when we have an "enforcer" on our bench, the game is noticeably cleaner than when he's not in the line-up. There's a lot less stick work, a lot less hacking and whacking. So fighting and the presence of an enforcer, even if he's only on the bench has a policing effect on the game and makes some guys think twice about taking a run at the other team's leading scorer.

It's just like having a bully on your block who picks on any kid who walks on the grass in front of his house; you will either be careful to walk on the sidewalk or take a different route to school. You may never actually fight the bully, but you respect (or fear) him and don't engage in conduct (walking on his grass) that will aggravate him. That's the same role an enforcer plays in hockey.

If you don't want to aggravate the other team's enforcer, play the game cleanly and respect his players and you'll never be confronted. But taunt him (like, "You don't look so tough to me"), or run his goalie, or two-hand slash his leading scorer in the back of the neck when the referee isn't looking, and you'll be dancing with him on your next shift and it won't be the polka.

I don't think we should only let angels play the game. Professional hockey players are extremely competitive, very intense, and highly motivated to win, and they will take advantage of every mistake, weakness, or careless play that they can and push the rules to the limit. The extremely competitive, very intense, and highly motivated players on the other team will sometimes take exception to this extreme competitiveness and intensity, and tempers will be lost and there will be confrontations, scuffles, and tussles.

Add that to the fact that the owners notice that often the only time fans stand during a game, other than to go out for an adult beverage, is when a fight breaks out. And usually the more aggressive the fighters, the greater the number of fans who get on their feet. Fighting will stay in professional hockey. It plays a role in the game and many fans love it.

JAY

When Dan says that he and my other sons didn't fight in youth hockey because they thought I would go over the boards to take them off the ice myself, they were right—I did mean it. I'll second what Dan said about there being absolutely no place in youth hockey for fighting, for a coach who condones it, or for a parent who thinks it's cute or macho. Period.

The only reasons why we have organized youth athletics in place is so kids can have fun, learn life lessons, and perhaps to keep off the street (and it kept my boys away from girls—for a while anyway). Fighting isn't fun, it teaches you the wrong lessons, and if you're going to fight, you might as well be on the street.

But if your goal is to make it to the NHL, perhaps there's a different reason not to fight. In an earlier chapter, we talked about what your chances are of making it to the NHL. I said they were about 1 in 3,333. That's the chances of a U.S. born player making any team's 24-man roster.

But, there's only one enforcer on some teams and none on others. If you expect to make it as a fighter, then you're trying to make only one spot that's available on each team instead of 24 and your chances diminish considerably. So as slim as your chances already are, they're even worse as a fighter. Besides, fighting is not allowed in college hockey, so your ability to fight isn't going to impress any college coaches, and as we said before—college is the route for most U.S. players to get to the NHL.

I never forgot what one coach said to his player who had gotten into a fight. After a good scolding, the player said, "What's the big deal, they fight all the time in the NHL." The coach replied, "When you can skate like an NHLer you can think about fighting like an NHLer."

So what do we think about fighting? In youth hockey, it's a bad idea. As we said earlier, youth hockey gives you a glimpse of what life is like. Fighting in hockey, like fighting in life, usually gets you nowhere.

32 WHAT IS A TYPICAL DAY LIKE FOR A PLAYER IN THE NHL?

BE CAREFUL WHAT YOU PRAY FOR.

—DAN

DAN

There are two kinds of typical days. The days when the team is playing at home and the days when the team is playing on the road.

Whether the team is playing at home or on the road, there are two other kinds of days. There are practice days and game days. On practice days at home, I get up around 7:30 A.M. and spend some time with my little boy, have some cereal, or a bagel, or both, and leave the house at about 9:00 A.M. for the rink. When I get to the rink, I check the results of the games played the night before and their effect on the standings. Then there might be treatment for an injury or a sore spot. Meanwhile, players wander in at their own pace, some coming early to hang out, others coming just in time to take care of business.

There is usually about a 20-minute spin on the stationary bike to get warmed up and then get dressed and hit the ice at about 11:00. There will be an hour skate. Sometimes it's a so-called "light skate" in which the goal is to keep the legs and the lungs in shape and skate line-for-line with the players who you will be skating with in the next game. Sometimes it's a "not-so-light skate." These usually happen if the coach feels some of the players slacked off in the previous game or didn't give the game plan their full attention. These kinds of practices can take the edge off your skates, make noodles of your legs, and have you sucking serious wind.

After the practice, there may be meetings with the coaches (they rarely call you in to tell you how great you played), or for the penalty killing or power play squads. There is also opportunity to cool down by riding the bike (again) and doing some reps on the weights. Some players will be back on the training table taking treatments or icing down some ache or pain while they ride the bike.

Occasionally there will be media types in the locker room who need to write something interesting about the team for their newspapers or the TV broadcasters who need to do features for their between-period shows and you may get tabbed to talk about how you tape your sticks or how you kill penalties. Sometimes ESPN or "Hockey2nite" will come around to talk about what you do in the summer or about one of your hobbies for one of their broadcasts.

You can usually leave the rink by about 1:00 or 1:30 P.M. and the rest of the day is yours to spend with your family or to do the chores that pile up while you're on the road (yes, NHL players have chores just like your fathers do). Sometimes there are promotional events that you need to attend, such as an autograph session at a Kmart, a radio interview, or a charity golf outing. Once I went to a Boston Garden restaurant and participated in a sandwich invention contest. I lost to Matt Johnson, but I made a darn good sammie!

Because we're in Los Angeles, we sometimes get to go to TV shows. I've been to the taping of "Coach" and met all the cast members, and I've been to the "Tonight Show." Once I took my mom and dad to the "Tonight Show" when Jerry Seinfeld was the guest. It was great. Players also get VIP treatment at restaurants and places like Universal Studios, which really impresses your brothers and sisters when they come to town. You see, the people at Universal Studios think I'm a member of an NHL team—a star. They don't know I'm really just Dan Bylsma from Grand Haven, Michigan! (And don't you tell them different, either.)

A typical game day starts the same but the skate is almost always a light skate. If you are not playing in the game (that's called being a scratch), you stay after the regular practice and play shinny or three-on-three with the other scratches and the coaches. This is so that you get somewhat the same conditioning that you would get if you were playing.

After practice there may be treatments or interviews, but I'm usually home by 12:00 P.M. I eat a substantial pre-game meal with lots of salad and carbohydrates—usually pasta of some kind or other. Then I take a two-hour, pre-game nap. That allows my body to relax and store up the energy from the pre-game meal. (I know this part sounds tough, but it's a job and someone has to do it!)

I'm usually at the rink by 5:00 P.M. and the pre-game ritual begins. First, we put on some high-energy music to help get us charged up. Then I make a careful check of my equipment to make sure the skates are sharpened the way I like it, enough sticks are ready, etc. Then perhaps there's more medical treatment or physical therapy. (Can you tell it's important to take care of your body?) Depending on how I feel, perhaps there's a trip to the bathroom to take care of business, a short spin on the stationary bike to get my legs warmed up, some stretching exercises, getting dressed, and hitting the ice for warm-ups.

Then there's the game, the reason behind all the preparation.

After the game, there's a brief time when the team is alone—no visitors, including the media—for a post-game discussion by the coaches (sometimes it's a discussion, sometimes it's a butt-chewing). It's also a time to get out of the skates and gear. Then the post-game ritual begins: talking to reporters (if you're a big star or if you scored); getting an ice pack or two or three for the sore spots, bruises, and aching muscles; a cooling down period, perhaps by riding the stationary bike (again); then medical attention or therapy, perhaps a whirlpool bath, maybe a soft tissue massage, and finally a shower and getting dressed. Usually I'm not out of the locker room for at least an hour, sometimes two hours, then it's out to a quiet restaurant or home for dinner.

For road trips, we fly on a chartered plane with very nice accommodations like leather seats that swivel and recline so you can lay flat and sleep, individual TV sets, and food that is typically like that in a very fine restaurant. We get to stay in very nice hotels, two to a room and usually with the same roommate all season. We have an 8:00 wake up and go to the hotel dining room for a buffet-style breakfast. Then we board a bus to the rink for a skate very much like the practices at our home arena. Of course, the team brings all its own equipment like skate sharpeners and medical supplies.

The game day routine is the same as when we are playing at home and usually we are bussed to the airport right after the game to fly home or to the next city that night. That's because it's hard to sleep right after the high energy of playing a game. So the plane ride gives you a chance to relax and then you can often sleep later the following morning rather than trying to get to sleep right after the game and getting up early in the morning to catch a plane.

On off days on the road, there is a team lunch after the morning skate and then players might take in a movie or relax by the pool with a book or a crossword puzzle. I get to read a lot of books and have worked a fair amount of crossword puzzles.

When you are on the road, you get a certain amount of money for meals. It allows you to go to good restaurants and eat in a way that is healthy for your body—a big breakfast before the morning skate and a big pasta dinner for lunch on game days, for example. As you might expect, I don't eat much pasta in the summer.

Speaking of summer, contrary to what you might think, a player who is conscientious will work as hard on his conditioning and strength training in the summer as he does during the season. Typically I take three weeks off and let my mind relax and my body begin to heal. I try to do a lot of fishing throughout the summer—trout fishing on the great trout streams in Michigan and salmon fishing on Lake Michigan. I also run my hockey schools. But after my three weeks off, I begin working out.

Physically, I do strength training every other day, alternating between upper body and lower body strength. So it's upper body on Tuesday and lower body on Thursday. On the days I don't do strength training, I run and work on foot speed. Sometimes my brothers like to imply that

I don't do anything in the summer, but I know they wouldn't like to follow me around and do what most professional hockey players and I do "on vacation."

Players are usually involved with some kind of physical therapy for chronic shoulder pain, knee injuries, back problems, or a wide assortment of other aches and pains that accumulate in a very physical sport over the 82 games of the regular season and, hopefully, more in the playoffs. One summer I needed to have my nose repaired, another summer it was a recurring shoulder problem, next summer it may be arthroscopy on my knees. And sooner or later, I'll have to have surgery on my elbows.

I was once asked during a guest appearance how many stitches I've received over my career. The answer prior to the 1999–2000 season was more than 550 in my face (and some of the resultant scars look like the stitches were put in by the Zamboni driver). Then I was asked how many broken bones I've had and the answer was 21. So while it can be a very glamorous life, and there are some very nice rewards, financial and otherwise, and most of us want to be here in the NHL more than anyplace else or doing anything else, there is a price each of us pays. Be careful what you pray for.

JAY

What's life like for the father of an NHLer? Well, I'm glad I don't have to be making ice ponds in our backyard anymore, or pay for the ice time and the gear!

I try to make sure I'm home to watch Dan's games on TV. Dan's mom keeps stats on how many shifts he takes, who scores, who gets scored on, etc. Quite often I will say to her, "That Number 21 looks a lot like our son Dan."

She will say, "Really? Number 21? On which team?" That's our little joke because after five seasons, it's still hard for us to believe we actually have a son who plays in the NHL.

33 HOW DID YOU GUYS MAKE YOUR BACKYARD ICE RINK?

IF YOU BUILD IT, HE WILL COME.

—*WILLIAM P. KINSELLA*

JAY

Over the years, a lot of people have asked us how we made all those ice ponds in our backyard. Because we've mentioned the advantages of having your own ice sheet to play on, we've decided to share our methods and some tricks we learned over 25 years of making them. We tried a lot of different methods and found this one works best and fastest for larger sheets (our ponds ranged from 35' × 70' to 70' × 120').

Area

Obviously, having a flat yard works best, but our method works well for backyards with small slopes as well. We found that a bit of work in the fall will be helpful. Mowing the lawn short at the end of the mowing season will prevent tufts of grass or weeds from growing up through the surface of the pond. Raking all the leaves out of the yard will help also. The value of this late fall maintenance will become clear later.

Equipment

A flexible ⅝"- or ¾"-diameter hose works best and you should equip the end with a gun-type nozzle. You will also need a large sturdy pail; a five-gallon lard bucket from a bakery works well. For clothes, a pair of waders, a waterproof jacket—preferably with a hood (we used a snowmobile suit we found at a garage sale for $5)— heavy rubber gloves with a pair of brown jersey gloves inside, and a ski mask will be worth the trouble to round them up. The waders needn't be leakproof as one might want for fishing; an old leaky pair will go a long way to keeping you dry and therefore warm. Don't skimp on the rubber gloves; get a large heavy duty pair for protection, then fit a pair of inexpensive brown jersey gloves inside for warmth. Have two pairs of jersey gloves and keep one pair on a warm-air register to put on when the first pair gets wet.

Preparation

Start with a good snow base—6" to 9" is best. If you don't have a snow base, the dark ground or grass will absorb heat from the sun and your pond will melt from the bottom up on a sunny 20°F day. The snow blocks out the sun and insulates the ice and your pond will last longer.

Pack the snow down as best you can. A snowmobile does a great job but only if you can turn it around past the area of the pond. If you try to turn it within the area of the pond, you will get ruts that will take some work to get rid of. Alternatively, a plastic sled loaded with kids (or a willing mother) pulled by an adult works nicely.

Laying the Ice Down

After the snow is packed down, begin to fog the snow with the finest spray or mist your hose nozzle will generate. Move about in a regular pattern (like a smaller oval path inside the larger oval of the pond) or better yet, if your pond is smaller, you may be able to spray the whole pond without walking on it. The trick here is to eliminate as many footprints in the snow under the ice as possible as they will need to be filled in later. Move as quickly as needed to allow as many droplets as possible to freeze as they hit the packed snow without laying or collecting in puddles on the snow. If the water droplets do not freeze when they land but collect or run, you are putting too much water down or you are not waiting long enough for the previous coat to fully set up. If you don't wear waders, you won't last long because the spray drifts if you have it adjusted properly and not all of it hits the pond. The rubber gloves get bonus points here, too.

Here's a hint: holding the nozzle to direct the spray upward allows some of the heat in the tap water to escape into the cold air and cool the water before it comes down. In no event should you allow the water to collect on the snow. Your goal here is to build an ever-thickening crust on top of the packed snow. The best time to do this is at night when the temperature is lowest and there is no sun. Obviously, the colder the weather, the more water you can fog on and the faster your progress will be. We used to take one-hour shifts beginning after supper and go as late into the night as Mom would allow (2:00 A.M.?). After two nights of this you should be able to walk on the pond without breaking through the crust.

When the crust will hold you, the next step is to take the five-gallon pail and fill it with fresh snow and then with water. Use this slush (let most of the water drain back into the pail before applying) to fill in the footprints you've made or places where the water insists on flowing through or any depressions or rough spots. Use this slush like you would use wet plaster to patch a hole in a wall: stick it down, press it in, smooth it out, and wipe away any excess water. Here the need for the rubber gloves is obvious.

Another night of fogging after the slush treatment and you will begin to see the ice surface develop and it will take on a mirror/sheet-like appearance. Do not be tempted to flood the pond—ever. With this fogging method you are putting layer upon layer down. Like plywood, it will be strong and it will resist cracking. After the third night, the best thing you can do is skate on it. Skating will shave all the bumps and ridges.

Maintenance

Each night, after all the fun, scrape the pond, repair any damage with slush, and re-fog it. Your goal here is to get as much of the ice shavings and snow off the ice as possible. Super wide, heavy scraper-type snow shovels will make the job go faster. This must be done *without fail*. If the weather should turn on you (to rain or a thaw) and you left the sheet dirty, and then it freezes, your pond will be ruined if not hard to skate on. If you are diligent in this maintenance each night, it will make life easier for you, even for shoveling the next day if you get an inch or two of snow overnight.

Some Hints

- This "fine spray" is best achieved using as much water pressure as you can muster coming out of the smallest hole in your nozzle. In other words, the valve at the house should be on full force and the nozzle closed down to make a mist or a fog of water. This will be easier to achieve if you have the larger diameter hose we suggested.
- If you work facing a spotlight, you will be able to watch the interaction of the water with

the surface, see how quickly the water is freezing, and know how soon you can put the next coat on.

● You have to be conscious of keeping your hose moving. If the host remains on the ice for any length of time, the heat from the water in the hose will melt down through your pond in the early stages. Just keep moving your entire length of hose if you can't keep it off the pond altogether. The hose can be a great leveler (trowel) if it happens to be snowing lightly as you're spraying; it works like a giant straight edge and fills in any cracks or ruts as you drag the hose over the wet snow/slush.

● If you happen to pack any leaves into the snow in your base, they will melt the ice around them with the first direct sunlight and make a hole. So keep leaves out of the snow in your base. Here's where getting the leaves out of your yard in the fall will be helpful. If you have any tufts of weeds or tall grass that stick up through the snow, they will also absorb the sunlight and heat up and melt the ice around them. That's why we suggest the short mowing.

● If it snows more than a dusting on the pond, you must scrape it off before you next fog. It's a big mistake to fail to do this because you will essentially have to start over to get that layer of now frozen slush fixed. Of course, if you get enough snow and can get it off evenly (like going around and around from the middle with a snow blower), it's a great material for side boards.

- Any cracks, leaf holes, or other damage is quickly fixed with a pail of slush used like plaster or cement. It works best if you let most of the water drain out before you lay it on at the beginning. If you have an inch of ice, this draining isn't so important.
- Painting lines in the ice is a mistake as the color will absorb the heat from the sun and you will have melting you don't want.
- Leaving your nets or pucks or shovels on the ice during a sunny day will also be a disaster. Black pucks, for example, will absorb the suns rays, heat up, and slowly melt down through the ice. It's the same with nets.
- With the fogging method we suggest, you don't need a perfectly flat surface. Our first pond had a slope of two feet from one corner to the far corner but with the fogging technique, the water freezes before it has a chance to run, so there are no rivulets, no melting through, and you get a mirrorlike finish.
- If you can help it, don't lay your pond over a septic tank as the warm water discharged from doing the wash or taking a shower heats the

ground above the tank and your pond will melt in that area from the bottom up.

🏒 I found that a gun-type nozzle, opened to a fine spray, with the trigger taped down to the desired "squeeze" is a good idea. It prevents accidentally shooting a stream into the snow creating a hole that will come back to haunt you, and no one will have to worry about what exactly is meant by a "fine spray" when they are doing this mind-numbing, bone-chilling endeavor hour after hour.

🏒 To prevent your hoses from freezing, if you can't take them into a heated shed or garage, turn the flow down to little more than a running trickle and prop the hose (so it sprays away, not down) on the top of a fence and let it run. Your hose won't freeze and you will create a wonderful ice sculpture that will last well into April.

Reviewing this almost makes me want to go out in the yard and get a pond going again. As I write this, we've got about nine inches of fresh powder and it's 15°F . . . wait a minute! What am I thinking?

You may wonder why flooding the pond is not recommended. There are several reasons. The most important is that the water coming out of your house will be 55°F at its coldest. That means in order for that water to freeze, its temperature has to drop more than

23°F. A single droplet is able to release its heat very quickly. A volume of water takes a long time and before it freezes, it will melt a lot of the snow or ice that it comes into contact with. You can test this out by taking an eye dropper and dropping one drop of cold tap water on a snowball. The snowball will freeze the drop of ice almost instantly. But if you pour a bucket of water on the snowball, it will damage the snowball if it doesn't melt it entirely.

Another reason why flooding is not recommended is that if you are able to contain the water and allow it to set up and freeze, you will have created a solid sheet of ice. This solid sheet will have a lot of internal tension and will crack at the first change in temperature, which happens a lot in winter. If you then re-flood the pond, water will stand on the ice, form a film of ice on the top, but the water underneath the film will seep through the cracks and you will have created air pockets that you will break through the first time you skate on it. It's not a nice surface to try to stick-handle on. The fogging method we prefer creates a surface that's as smooth as glass, resists cracking, and has no air pockets.

Building and maintaining an ice pond is tedious and usually done in difficult conditions. You stand in the sub-freezing cold by the hour while the rest of the family is sitting in front of a toasty fireplace. But I have never regretted a moment of it. Our ponds were the scenes of great games, great competition, and great family times. We would suspend bedtimes and play until I ran out of gas or Mom finally turned the lights out. Then we would sit in our makeshift locker room in our basement and watch the steam rise off our jerseys as we cooled down and reflected on the games we had played or the moves we had tried in our endless games of showdown. Not only were these great family times; frankly, it's the hockey that we played in the backyard that got Dan to the NHL.

34 WHAT IS SUCCESS?

THERE ARE MANY HARD AND FAST RULES FOR SUCCESS, BUT THE
TROUBLE IS ALL ARE HARD AND NONE ARE FAST.

—AUTHOR UNKNOWN

DAN

There are so many factors outside of your control that success cannot be guaranteed. But what you can guarantee is that when your chance comes, when doors open, when you are presented with an opportunity, you will be ready to make the most of it. You can condition yourself for success. In fact, eventually success will be ordinary and not extraordinary.

The most important thing in achieving success is making that goal the most important thing in your life, making it a Number One priority. Your goal can be becoming a better student, a better reader, better at math, becoming the first chair in your section in the band, or becoming the best penalty killer on your team or in the league.

And when your goal becomes an important thing in your life, you will slowly be tapping into the energy and motivation you need to realize your goal.

If you envision where you are going and set a goal, you can then devise a plan and chart your progress. The discipline of setting the goal and planning, in and of itself, sets you on a course. That alone will provide you with motivation and the energy necessary for progress.

The second step is to evaluate what you need to change in order to achieve your goal. What are your strengths and weaknesses? What do you need to develop in order to get to your Number One priority? For me, if Dan Bylsma wants to become a better hockey player; he needs to be quicker, a better skater, and handle the puck better. Those are the three weaknesses that he can improve on. His strengths are his intelligence, determination, strength, and hard work. How am I going to build on and use my strengths and improve my weaknesses? This is the process of honest evaluation. How can I get better?

The third step is setting daily, weekly, and monthly goals and a plan to achieve them. What action will I take to better develop my strengths and improve my weaknesses? The steps I take must be done on a regular, if not daily, basis. Then, assuming the plan is carried out, I have the satisfaction that today I did what I could to improve myself, to accomplish my goal. Today I have been in the business of making myself better.

If you follow that routine, what you will be doing is conditioning yourself for success—and you will be achieving it on a daily basis. Success then is no longer extraordinary; it is ordinary because you attained it yesterday, the week before, and the month before. And soon you will expect yourself to be goal-oriented everyday. You will be in the process each day of making yourself a better person than you were the day before. Your next year will be the best year so far because you're in the process of making yourself better. You're not guaranteeing yourself success. What you will be guaranteeing is that you will be prepared when the next opportunity comes. You will be ready to step through that door of opportunity. It is a conscious process.

The final goal, more often than not, is not just one step away. What enables us to achieve higher levels is the reevaluation process. This became evident to me when I made it to the NHL. Making it to the NHL was my lifelong goal and dream. So powerful was my dream that I didn't think about what I might do after the NHL; all my goals were just to get there.

When I finished college and was in the ECHL, my goal was to make it to the AHL or the IHL. During the two and one half years I played in the AHL and the IHL, my goal was to make it to "The Show." Then in December of my fourth year as a professional I received the call-up phone call to play in the NHL. I had breakfast with my mom who was in Milwaukee to see the IHL game I was supposed to be in that night. I called my wife and siblings. I remember getting on the plane to Los Angeles and walking into the Great Western Forum (the Kings' home arena). It was the biggest high of my life.

However, as soon as I put on my skates and went on the ice, I realized that I wasn't prepared. I hadn't set my goals for anything higher than just making it. When I got there and experienced it, I thought, "If I would've known what it was going to be like, I would have trained harder." There is no equivalent of a flight simulator for the NHL.

I struggled through two practices and two games. I think I did well for myself, but mentally I was out of place and unprepared. Who was I and what was I doing here? Was I really on the same bench with Wayne Gretzky and playing against the Toronto Maple Leafs? When I was sent back down to the minors, I sat in my apartment with my wife and felt relieved to be back in Phoenix. Los Angeles was scary. Phoenix was safe. The Los Angeles experience was awesome, but mentally I wasn't sure that I was ready to play at that level.

When I got to the rink the next morning, my coach, Rob Laird, called me into his office and congratulated me. "I know that you beat the odds of getting into the NHL. Nobody gave you a chance and you surprised everybody. But I didn't just call you in here to just congratulate you and say, 'Great career.' I want to challenge you to take the next step. The step beyond just making it. Now I want you to evaluate what you saw, evaluate where you are now, and work even harder than you have ever done before. I want you to know that I believe and I know you believe that you can stay there, you can excel there. But you need to dedicate yourself at getting back in the NHL and staying there. It isn't just going to happen and you know what you need to work on. You need to challenge yourself more than you ever have before."

It took me about a week to let what Coach Laird said sink in, to realize what he was telling me. He was saying that I had achieved this dream that had been against all odds and realistically beyond my grasp. But the success I achieved in getting to "The Show" was only a beginning to something better if I was able to refocus and set new goals. Success was not standing in the NHL in a pair of skates. Real success could be achieved again if I took the challenge, set the goal, and dedicated the time and the effort to make myself a better player so that if I got the opportunity to play again I would belong there.

Success is not just making it to the NHL; success is a continuous process. It's a continuum. It happens daily. When you make yourself better on a daily basis, when you set goals and achieve them, you are achieving success. It is not extraordinary. You do not all of a sudden achieve a huge amount of success the day you make it to the NHL or reach whatever goal you have set for yourself. To get there, you have to have been achieving success all along. You were just making yourself ready for the chance and when the chance came you were able to take advantage of it. Taking advantage of it means to reevaluate, refocus, and rededicate so that when you get there you can stay there. When you get there, you should be ready mentally to say "I belong here."

That was my challenge. I had to challenge myself to re-evaluate. What did I see in the NHL? How hard were the guys working, what was their skill level, and what do I need to do to belong there? And I had to rededicate and refocus. That is the last and the biggest key to being successful. Once you have improved and reached your goals, you need to reevaluate where you are going, how good you are becoming, what are you good at, and what do you need to work on. Then you can go about setting new goals and achieving them. This is truly how the successful road (not the road to success) is traveled.

I often hear people talking about successful people in terms of being lucky or fortunate. There is a notion that the things that make them successful are things that we just don't have available to us. There *must* be a success gene and it is stronger in successful people, weaker in the rest of us. Or perhaps it's luck or being in the right place at the right time. I contend that success more often comes through this process of setting goals, working hard to accomplish the goals, and then reevaluating where you are and where you want to go from where you are. In the main it is not luck. It is preparation. It is being ready for the next opportunity when it comes.

Being successful is when opportunity and preparation meet. When you are prepared to walk through the door of success, you are lucky. To those who aren't prepared and aren't ready, the success of others may be perceived as luck. They don't realize that the harder you work the luckier you become. In hockey, we have a saying about that: "If you work hard enough, the puck will follow you."

If success is a continuum, then it is not signified by an accomplishment, it is the process of accomplishing noticeable improvement. Success is not something you will have one day, but did not have the day before. Successful means being "full of successes." Thinking of success in that way, it is not something that only Michael Jordan or Wayne Gretzky or someone else with better genes can attain. I can be successful as a player, as a student, as a coach, as a husband, as a father.

My father used to say to us kids, "to rise above the sea of mediocrity [the average kid] takes only a little extra effort." You need only to move into the percentage of people that work hard and care. If I have successes in lots of little ways I become full of success—success-ful. You can be too. Starting today.

35 DON'T STOP DREAMING!

WHAT THE MIND CAN CONCEIVE, THE MAN CAN ACHIEVE.

—*AUTHOR UNKNOWN*

DAN

Don't stop dreaming. Reach for the stars (or the Kings or the Ducks or the Red Wings). And if you want it and work for it as hard as you dream for it, you may wake up in the NHL some day. I did and it was a very, very good feeling.

JAY

It takes three things to make your dream come true: talent, hard work, and perseverance. And the greatest of these is not talent.

36 | *A FINAL THOUGHT*

CHARACTER IS THE FINAL DECISION TO REJECT WHATEVER IS
DEMEANING TO ONESELF OR TO OTHERS AND WITH
CONFIDENCE AND HONESTY TO CHOOSE THE RIGHT.

—*GENERAL ARTHUR G. TRUDEAU*

DAN

Throughout the book my father and I have tried to show you that the ability to play a sport well is not the only thing necessary for being successful in it. Both of us have learned that character is a very important part of making the athlete successful. It may be the most important part.

Remember that I said when college coaches called my General Manager in Juniors, the first question they asked was, "What were his grades or college entrance exam scores?" Well, the second question was, "What kind of a kid is he?" They were asking about my character.

I hope when the college coach calls to ask your General Manager what kind of a kid you are, words like "lazy," "does just enough to get by," "inconsiderate," "selfish," "doesn't listen to the coach," "smokes," "got into some trouble with the law" are not the words that come to your GM's mind.

I hope your General Manager can use words like "hard working," "leader," "coachable," "team player," "no trouble off the ice," and "a credit to our program." I want your GM to be able to say "This is a young person of character" and "This young man has his head screwed on straight." If he can't, life after hockey will come very soon, most likely sooner than you might want.

The importance of having one's head screwed on straight was never clearer to me than when I finally arrived in the NHL. As a new player in the league it was easy to be in awe of the players, the arenas, the fans, the charter planes, the fancy hotels, and the big cities that were all a part of "The Show." I had to stay focused on hockey while dealing with the glitter and glamour both on and off the ice.

Finding your place on the team is another challenge. Knowing who to talk to, what to say, where to go, and how to act is an important factor when trying to settle into the social atmosphere of the team. Even more important is being able to relax and concentrate on playing your best hockey every game. The problem is even more difficult when you are a young player or a rookie because many of the veterans have formed friendships and tend to stick together. If you do things to put you in disfavor with the veterans, they can ruin you. For example, say you are a high draft pick and come to camp as a rookie full of self-importance and show little respect for veteran jour-neyman players whose names you don't recognize. Those veterans can make life miserable and worse.

Here's how it can work. The rookie knows how impor-tant it is to make a good impression during practice. He is second in line to do a drill and a veteran is in front of him. Instead of taking off to take a pass and do the drill when his turn comes, the veteran suddenly skates to the rear of the line leaving the rookie (who was not expecting it to be his turn) standing there like a dummy. The whis-tle blows, the drill comes to a stop, the rink becomes quiet, and the coach gets in the rookie's face for screwing up the drill. Little things like that, done to fracture an inflated ego, can deflate a career.

I cannot stress enough how important it is to have your head screwed on straight—to be a person of character. The pressures you need to handle at the college and pro-fessional levels—uncertainty about your career, dealing with reporters, and the fans when suddenly you are seen as a big hero; peer pressure; the pressure to perform; slumps in your performance; the inability to sense your place in the order of things; and yes, the lack of social skills—have ruined more careers than you might think.

And what do you call the ability to handle these pres-sures, to sense your place, to have a moral compass and social graces? It's called character. And as we said earlier, character is a very important part of success in sports, maybe the *most* important part.

If you are tempted to challenge this wisdom, consider all the athletes who can no longer play the game they love so much because they lacked character. Charged with assaults, drug use, alcohol abuse, gambling, bankruptcy, or other problems, they had to leave professional sports. And for every one you can name there are dozens more whose lack of character brought their careers to a stop before they ever made it to "The Show."

So you want to play in the NHL? Keep on dreaming, keep on working, persevere, and, along the way, prepare yourself for life by becoming a person of character.

AFTERWORD

If you are a young hockey player or the parent or coach of a young player and have a question about youth hockey, E-mail your questions or comments to *questions@danbylsma.com*. You can see the questions that other kids and parents have asked and our answers on the Question and Answer page of Dan's website: *www.danbylsma.com*.

We welcome comments about the book. E-mail your comments to *opinions@danbylsma.com*.